D1196939

VOLUME II

SEASONS
OF THE
LORD

Bible-centered Devotions on

Resurrection
and
Glory

HARPER JUBILEE BOOKS

VOLUME II

SEASONS
OF THE
LORD

Bible-centered Devotions on

Resurrection
and
Glory

HERBERT
LOCKYER

HARPER & ROW, PUBLISHERS

New York, Hagerstown, San Francisco, London

SEASONS OF THE LORD. VOLUME II. Copyright © 1977 by Herbert Lockyer. All rights reserved. Printed in the United States of America. No part of this book may be used or reproduced in any manner whatsoever without written permission except in the case of brief quotations embodied in critical articles and reviews: For information address Harper & Row, Publishers, Inc., 10 East 53rd Street, New York, N.Y. 10022. Published simultaneously in Canada by Fitzhenry & Whiteside Limited, Toronto.

FIRST EDITION

A HARPER JUBILEE GIANT ORIGINAL

Designed by Eve Kirch Callahan

Library of Congress Cataloging in Publication Data

Lockyer, Herbert.
  Seasons of the Lord.
  (Harper jubilee books; HJG 02-05)
  CONTENTS: v. 1. Bible-centered devotions on purity and hope.—v. 2. Bible-centered devotions on resurrection and glory.—v. 3. Bible-centered devotions on fulfillment and splendor. [etc.]
  1. Bible—Meditations—Collected works.
I. Title.
BS483.5.L6   242'.08   76-9998
ISBN: 0-06-065266-7

77 78 79 80 81 8 7 6 5 4 3 2 1

Contents

Gaiety and Glory

Preface

The leading month of the second quarter of the year's circle is truly nature's debutant, coming to us with all the beautiful garments which poets have vied one another to describe. April, the womb of nature, opens with life as trees break their buds to bear golden leaves. Resurrection is seen in the carpet of primroses, violets, and spring flowers covering the earth. April's lady comes forth with all her glory to praise the Creator who furnished her. What a fitting time of the year this is to illustrate the victory of the Rose of Sharon who rose again, alive forevermore.

The poet Keats spoke of the merriment of May because of the mirthful singing of the birds, the livery of green, and the beauty of the gardens. Loveliness and vitality are implied by Shakespeare as he spoke of May's new-fangled mirth. How fascinating also it is to watch the economy of growth. The silent agencies of nature seek to perfect the fruits and flowers of the earth—a lesson for our hearts to learn in growing, not only to grace but to graciousness.

When we reach the closing month of the second quarter of the year, the green woods laugh with the voice of joy completing the circle of spring. There is a gaiety in the hearts of all true lovers of nature when June comes around. Every prospect seems to please, and only humankind is vile. "Rejoice, and again I say, rejoice" is the injunction of Scripture.

x

RESURRECTION

O, how this spring of love
resembleth
The uncertain glory of an
April day.

    —William Shakespeare,
      The Two Gentlemen of Verona

Each to His Great Father Bends

"Our Father which art in heaven." *Matthew 6:9.*

The Bible abounds in illustrations of the tenderheartedness of God. We know of his loving, kind, and understanding nature as our heavenly Father, whose gentleness makes him great. Jesus not only exhibited fatherly tenderness and forgiveness when, as he died, he prayed for his enemies. Isaiah depicted him as the everlasting Father, or Father of eternity. *Father!* What a precious portrait of the Lord this is, manifested in his love, carrying him to great lengths to extricate his wayward children out of trouble. All strength, wisdom, and provision are his as the Father of the fatherless.

While, in the sense of creation, he is the Father of us all, we cannot look up into his face and speak to him as our Father in heaven unless his beloved Son is our personal Savior. The privileged relationship of sonship is based upon regeneration (John 1:11–13). Only by the spirit of adoption can we cry, "Abba, Father!"

Are you certain that God is *your* Father through faith in his Son? If he is your heavenly Father, then rest in his fatherly pity and provision, singing at all times, "I know my heavenly Father knows." He can never forget his own, neglect their concerns, or turn a deaf ear to the needs and requests of his beloved, blood-bought children. His fatherly love is infinite and will remain fixed on us forever. Having loved us out of our sin to himself, he will love us unto the end. May we be found sharing the Father's compassion, displayed in the gift of his Son, for a sinful and sinning race.

In Mystery Our Soul Abides

"Now we see through a glass, darkly," *1 Corinthians 13:12.*

We can couple with Matthew Arnold's phrase, used above as the title of our meditation, the line of Shakespeare in *King Lear*, "And take upon 's the mystery of things." Paul reminded us that with our finite minds we cannot fully understand the significance of so many things our infinite God permits. "Now we see in a mirror dimly—or in a middle" (1 Cor. 13:12, RV).

Scientists used to write about the "Riddle of the Universe," but are there not a good many riddles in the little universe of your life and mine? Jesus said to Peter, "What I do you do not realize now; but you shall understand hereafter" (John 13:7). Often we are at a loss to account for many of the tears and trials in our Lord's dealings with us. Yet amid "the mystery of things" we must rest in the Lord's promise that we shall know hereafter. We must take comfort from the fact that heaven will explain the mysteries—"Then face to face." Said Paul of the paradise of Revelation, "Then shall we know."

When we see him who never makes a mistake or takes a wrong turning, then problems will be solved and all the trying dispensations of divine providences accounted for. Meantime, let us acknowledge the right of our all-wise Father to conceal the cause of his working until he has fully accomplished his designs. An unknown writer said:

> *I cannot read His future plans; but this I know:*
> *I have the smiling of His face, and all the refuge*
> *   of His grace,*
> *While here below.*

As Sentinels to Warn the Immortal Souls

"Give them warning from me." Ezekiel 3:17–19.

Although the *sentinels* Christopher Marlowe referred to are "the angels on the walls of heaven," those of us who are the Lord's should ever function as heaven-sent sentinels, warning immortal souls of their peril if they persist and die in sin. There are no more solemn words in the whole of Scripture than those in which Ezekiel is given his commission to warn the godless of the judgment awaiting them. The prophet was to stand before them in God's stead and tell the wicked of the dire consequences of their iniquity. If as a watchman he failed in his grim task, then the blood of the godless would be upon his own soul. Out he must go and watch for souls as one that must give an account of his stewardship. Only thus could the sentinel deliver himself (Ezek. 3:19).

We often read of the prophets being laden with a *burden*, the nature of which was the perfect fulfillment of a divine commission. Have we a burden for the lost around us? As God's representatives, are we warning sinners to flee from the wrath to come? Does the eternal hopelessness of the sinner apart from Christ constrain us to give ourselves, unceasingly, to the unpleasant task of warning the wicked of their doom? Are we beseeching them in God's stead to be reconciled to him?

If only ours could be a passionate passion for souls. How terrible it is to realize that they may be souls in hell who might have been delivered from such eternal condemnation and despair if only we had been more faithful in warning the immortal of their fate in their final rejection of Christ! Tell some perishing soul *today* that Jesus died to save from sin and hell.

His Commands Are Enablings

"Faithful is He who calls you, and He will also bring
it to Pass." *1 Thessalonians 5:24*, ASB.

One of the most attractive aspects of the divine character is that whatever God commands he is able to supply. What he asks for, he gives, for his commands are his enablings. Paul reminded the Thessalonians that God desired their entire sanctification in the light of Christ's return—a state of soul absolutely impossible if left to themselves to produce it. So there came hope in the assertion that the one demanding such holiness would bring it to pass.

Augustine said, "Give what Thou commandest then command what Thou wilt!" To Israel of old came the command of the Lord, "Keep my judgments and do them." But power to obey came from him who said, "I am the Lord your God" (Ezek. 20:19). In such a relationship we have all necessary resources to fulfill what God requires of us. The order to walk in his statutes and keep his judgments would fill us with despair if we were left to our own ability to obey it. But when we remember that the Lord is our God and that he is the one who "worketh in us, both to will and do of his good pleasure," then we do not faint or give way to discouragement.

When we are wholly yielded to the Lord, he accomplishes in us, for us, and through us all he requires of us. How blessed we are when we discover that what God orders, he offers! Who among us could fill the order, "Be ye holy," if left to ourselves to manufacture such holiness? But what God seeks, he supplies—"For I am holy" (I Peter 1:16). Thus the holiness which is *to* the Lord is a holiness which is first *from* the Lord who is "the hidden source of every precious thing."

Plain Living and High Thinking

"Let them give us pulse to eat and water to drink."
Daniel 1:12.

Four lines from Wordsworth's "In London" are worthy of notice:

Plain living and high thinking are no more:
The homely beauty of the good old cause
Is gone; our peace, our fearful innocence,
And pure religion breathing household laws.

An unknown Englishman of a bygone century wrote, "I should be spare of sleep, sparer of diet, and sparest of time, that when the days of eating, drinking, clothing and sleeping shall be no more, I may eat of my Saviour's hidden manna, drink of the new wine in my Father's Kingdom, and inherit that rest which remaineth for the people of my God for ever and ever."

Plain living aids the body as well as the mind. With Daniel and his three friends, plain living resulted, not only in high thinking, but in a physical beauty and fitness surpassing those who dined off the rich fare of the king's table. Seasons of fasting, not only from food but from bodily pleasures that would ensnare us, are good for body and soul. Often when the apostles prayed, they fasted. Paul was *in fastings often.* Spiritual giants down the ages set themselves against the undue indulgence of the body in eating and drinking. They knew that nothing was more certain to befog and darken and blunt the mind. Thus abstinence fitted them for the lofty and sublime delights of fellowship with heaven.

Let us beware of overmuch restfulness and ease in sleep. Let us guard ourselves against the sloth and spiritual darkness engendered by over-indulgence. It is better to eat to live than to live to eat. *High living* is a decided barrier to *living on high.*

When from Earth the Fourth Descended

"The form of the fourth is like the Son of God."
Daniel 3:25.

In the early part of the nineteenth century W. Savage Landor wrote about the *fourth* dignitary, meaning the sovereign, George IV, with whom, Landor said, "God be praised, the George is ended!" But the *fourth* seen by the three Hebrew youths was a heavenly king whose reign will never end. Those courageous young men came to learn that there is no fire so fierce that the king of glory himself will not bear the heat and glow by their side. To Shadrach, Meshach, and Abed-nego, being near the furnace meant being near the Lord. When the fire was at its fiercest, he was there as their protector.

In our time science magnifies physical power and talks much about the survival of the fittest. But the fiery furnace proves that often the weakest in the eyes of the world have the secret of true survival. Christ has all power in heaven and on earth to rescue and deliver his persecuted, despised children. One of the old divines said that "every Christian is a Christ-enclosed one." How true this is! "When thou walkest through the fire, thou shalt not be burned" (Isa. 43:2). Christ bears the heat of the furnace flames every time.

Whether our furnace is sickness, poverty, temptation, misapprehension by others, or spiritual desolation, "the fourth . . . like the Son of God" is in it to protect and provide. When those three Hebrew youths were thrust into the furnace, the *fourth* was already there, waiting to welcome and console his valiant yet despised witnesses. Our blessed assurance is that whatever our lot, the mystic fourth is ever at our side as companion and deliverer.

Short Weight

"Thou are weighed in the balances, and art found wanting."
Daniel 5:27.

Scales are everywhere. We meet them in drugstores, restaurants, and fruit and candy shops, and almost every bathroom has a miniature scale to tell if we are keeping our weight down. In fact, our weight has become a matter of great concern, and all kinds of exercises and diets are prescribed to remove those extra pounds. Inspectors visit businesses and warehouses where scales are used to check whether the weights and measures are correct. Often heavy fines are imposed on salesmen guilty of selling food at short weight.

Evidently God is the heavenly inspector who has his standard measure to check whether any come short of his glory. Few, however, are willing to be weighed in God's balances. Belshazzar stepped on the scales and was found wanting. In our day the scales of accepted human morality are more popular, but the standards by which our hearts and lives are to be judged fall short of divine standards. A life may be moral, according to the highest earthly estimation, yet be sadly wanting—underweight —when weighed in the balance of the sanctuary. God's message to Belshazzar was, "The God in whose hand thy breath is, and whose are all thy ways, hast thou not glorified" (Dan. 5:23). Here then is the correct and only standard by which our hearts are to be weighed.

In his great sermon "Weighed in the Balances" the famous evangelist Dwight L. Moody used the Ten Commandments as weights by which to test ourselves. These and the various commands of the Lord Jesus are scales by which we are to try our weight if we want to know whether we are giving God good measure. As "the children of men are deceitful upon weights" (see Ps. 62:9), may our standards be true.

9

Surety Secure

"Jesus has become the guarantee of a better covenant."
Hebrews 7:22, ASV.

What a deep truth there is in Shakespeare's *Troilus and Cressida*:

> *. . . The wound of peace is surety,*
> *Surety secure.*

The wounds of the Prince of Peace secured a perfect surety for all who believe. If a sizable loan is required from a bank, those negotiating the loan want to know what security or collateral can be offered. Some guarantee equivalent of the value of the loan required must be available.

Is it not blessed to know that Jesus placed himself as our collateral, surety, bondsman? Is it not wonderful that, having no security of our own to offer, we can yet draw as much as we like on heaven's bank as long as we present our surety's name and merits? Did he not pledge himself as our security when he said, "Whatsoever ye shall ask in my name, that will I do" (John 14:13)?

With such infinite resources at our disposal there is no need whatever for spiritual impoverishment. Yet when needs arise, we lack the assurance that our heavenly collateral is more than sufficient. We are not altogether confident that the one who declared that "the silver and the gold are mine" (Hag. 2:8) is able to foot our bill. So we struggle on with so little, living too often as spiritual paupers, with such wealth at our disposal. Then, to think of it, what we draw on the bank of heaven is never a loan! Coming, in all our need to our surety, he willingly grants us an outright gift, all we ask of him.

Everything from A to Z

> "I am Alpha and the Omega, the beginning and the end, the
> first and the last." *Revelation 22:13 (see also 1:8, 21:6).*

I remember seeing over the window of a store trading in all kinds of merchandise the sign, "We sell everything from A to Z." Three times over Jesus referred to himself as Alpha and Omega in describing his all-sufficiency. These two titles constitute the first and last letters of the Greek alphabet, hence our Lord's application, "I am the first and the last." But he is not only our *A* and *Z*; he is also everything in between. Whether we think of creation, revelation, redemption, or personal experience, Jesus is "the beginning and the end." None is before him as *A*, and none can follow as *Z*.

Can we truthfully confess that he is everything from *A* to *Z* in our daily lives? When it comes to our desires, plans, and ambitions, is he the beginning and the end? Is everything inspired by his Spirit and undertaken for his glory? "In the beginning, God." "Man's chief end is to glorify God" (*Shorter Catechism*). What tranquillity is ours, and how life is made radiant with his provision when Jesus is all and in all to us! To have him answer to the whole of the alphabet of life is to spell out the language of heaven. How expressive of him as our *A* to *Z* are these lines of the English poet F. W. H. Myers in "St. Paul":

> *Yea, through life, death, through sorrow*
> *and through sinning,*
> *Christ shall suffice me, for He hath sufficed.*
> *Christ is the end, for Christ was the beginning*
> *Christ the beginning, for the end is Christ.*

Paul makes it clear that Jesus, who is before all things and in whom all things hold together, must have the first and last place in everything (Col. 1:15–19). He must be sanctified as Lord in the heart.

The Only Free Men Are the Only Slaves

"Paul, a servant of Jesus Christ." Romans 1:1.

The word Paul used for *servant* is given as "bond servant" and literally means "slave." In the apostle's day slaves abounded throughout the Roman Empire, slavery being countenanced in a most despotic and cruel form. But Paul took the term and ennobled it and would have us know that the saints are, or should be, the slaves of Jesus Christ. Thus William Cowper's phrase is apt, for the believer, freed from the penalty and dominion, is free and as such is bonded to the deliverer. He wrote in "The Winter Evening":

> *He is the freeman whom the truth sets free,*
> *And all are slaves beside.*

But they are slaves in the wrong sense.

Jesus was sold for thirty pieces of silver, the price paid for a common slave. But he came as the love-slave of heaven. While on earth he was subservient to the Father in all things. "Not my will but thine be done" (Luke 22:42). Like his Master, Paul looked upon himself as being harnessed to the chariot of the Lord and thus spoke of himself as a slave and a prisoner of the Master he dearly loved and so loyally served. Proudly he could boast, in the words of an unknown author:

> *A prisoner of Jesus Christ,*
> *Love's handcuffs neither cut nor chafe.*
> *I am the freest man in Rome*
> *All sins forgiven, for ever safe.*

The question you must answer is, Am I Christ's slave or the slave of sin? You cannot be the slave of both at the same time.

God . . . Ordains for Each One Spot

"He which was ordained of God." Acts 10:42.

The one spot Rudyard Kipling felt God had ordained for him was his beloved Sussex. Although "God gives all men the earth to love" and "for each one spot" and "each to his choice," which for the poet was "Sussex by the sea," God ordains not only *where* we live but *how* we live. Jesus speaks of ordaining his own to function in the world as fruit-bearers (John 15:16).

In our basic verse Peter spoke of Jesus as one ordained of God for a specific mission. When do you think he received his divine ordination? Was it not in a past eternity when he gladly offered himself as the Savior of the world? Peter called attention to the twofold obligation of the ordained Christ, namely, to be the judge of the living and the dead and to give remission of sins.

No wonder that as Peter spoke thus of Jesus, the Holy Spirit fell with a marked effect on those hearing such a message. The Christ-honoring spirit ever blesses the full testimony of the sent one of God who realized to the full his ordination vows. Usually we limit the term *ordination* to those entering the ministry or some church office, but Jesus says of all believers, "I have ordained you." The tragedy is that there are those ordained of men who were never divinely ordained. Are you the Lord's? Although you are not among the number wearing clerical garb —a symbol of religious ordination—yours is the ordination of the pierced hands of him who has saved you and set you aside to serve him fruitfully.

From Whom All Good Counsels Do Proceed

"His name shall be called . . . Counsellor." Isaiah 9:6.

Many collects of the Anglican church are rich in spiritual significance. An evening one from which I have taken the title of this meditation reads, "From whom all holy desires, all good counsels, and all just works do proceed."

In English law a QC is a Queen's Counsellor and represents high legal knowledge and authority. Isaiah declared that we are privileged to have the heavenly king himself as our counsellor. The first two names, *Wonderful* and *Counsellor*, are sometimes linked together and read, "The wonder of a Counsellor." And truly the Lord is "wonderful in counsel" (Isa 28:29). Such is his perfection in this realm that it is said of him, "Who hath been his counsellor?" (Isa. 40:13; Rom. 11:34). Court counsellors sometimes err or change their decisions, but our kingly counsellor gives verdicts that stand forever (Prov. 19:21).

When a case comes up in law courts, there are opposing counsellors, one defends the accused, and another prosecutes him. There is no counsel, however, against the Lord, for his case against those he accuses can never be refuted (Prov. 21:30). He is ever just and right in his decisions and judgments. Would that we could always accept the immutable, strong counsel of him who cannot err! (Jer. 32:19; Heb. 6:17). With James G. Small let us ever follow the advice of:

> *So wise a counsellor and guide,*
> *So mighty a Defender!*

Is it not encouraging to know that our heavenly counsellor has never lost a case?

An Ever-welcome Visitor

"What is man . . . that thou visitest him?" Psalm 8:4.

Some visitors are always welcome, and once with us we wish they would prolong their stay. Others are not so welcome, and the sooner they leave, the better, for they bore us by their company and conversation. Have you ever thought of the Lord as a visitor whose visits are most gratefully appreciated by those who love him? But there are others to whom his visits are unwanted, not because he is not the best of company, but because of their hatred for what he has to say. When in the hour of your salvation Jesus knocked at the door of your heart and asked, "May I come in?" he did not enter as a visitor, but as one who wanted to live with you or, to use his own phrase, "make his abode with you." Presently, your heart is his home, and when you reach the end of the road, you will be at home with him in heaven.

It is somewhat surprising how much the Bible has to say about the visits the Lord and his angels have paid to humans here on the earth. When he visited the sin of his people upon them, they were not pleased. Yet how warmly was his visit received when he came down to deliver them (Exod. 13:19). We Gentiles would have been of all men most miserable had he not visited us (Acts 15:14). A dreadful day of visitation awaits a godless world. Do we welcome the privilege of opening the door to him every morning, as Job 7:18 says we should? Once the door is opened to receive him, he closes the door behind him and becomes the abiding companion, promising never to leave us. We reflect on an unknown writer's words:

> *Come, not to find, but make this troubled heart*
> *A dwelling worthy of Thee as Thou art.*

It Is the Lord's Passover

"Christ our passover is sacrificed for us." 1 Corinthians 5:7.

The Passover, although still observed by the Jews, is no longer a *feast* but a *figure*, even Christ himself. The origin of the Passover is typical of Christ in many ways.

For instance, the lamb had to be without blemish; Christ was holy. The lamb had to be slain; Christ died for us. The blood had to be applied; Christ must be appropriated by faith. The blood instituted a perfect protection from judgment; Christ, by his finished work, affords eternal security for all who are blood-washed. Further, the feast itself answers to Christ as the Bread of Life. The Jews had the Passover; the church has the Lord's Supper.

What a great phrase that is—When I see the blood, I will pass over you! Is Christ your Passover in this respect? Is his blood upon you and your children? Paul enforced his appeal for separation from sin and sinners by using the illustration of Christ, sacrificed as our Passover. The Jews kept the feast with unleavened bread; so must we, not only for seven days, but for all our days. The whole life of a Christian must be a Feast of unleavened bread. The old leaven must be purged out. As those redeemed by Christ's precious blood we must be without guilt in our conduct toward God and humankind. The willing sacrifice of God's lamb at Calvary is the strongest argument for purity and sincerity.

The solemn question for each heart is, Am I sheltered by his blood? Critics and cynics may scoff at the necessity of being washed in blood, but apart from the covering his ruby blood offers, we have no hope of salvation here or in heaven hereafter.

When the Prince of Glory Died

"Ye killed the Prince of life." *Acts 3:15.*

Every lover of the Bible knows that apparent contradictions abound. I say *apparent*, for truth cannot contradict itself. The text before us is a case in point. They *killed* the Prince of *life*, but life is indestructible. Because Jesus came as the *Prince* of life, how could he, the eternal one, be put to death? Yet such is the mystery of the cross that he who said "I am . . . the life" died in agony and shame. Peter in his sermon contrasts the death of the Prince of life with Barabbas, the murderer who took life. Jesus, who came that men might have life, was the bestower of life; Barabbas was the destroyer of life. As the Prince of life Jesus' own life was so princely. With his disregard for life there was no nobility about the character of Barabbas.

Now alive forevermore, the crucified Prince proclaims that we can have life and have it more abundantly. Apart from him there is no life. If he who is our life is not within the heart as Savior and Lord, then spiritual death reigns. The tragedy is that multitudes prefer such a state of death, resulting ultimately in a condition of eternal death, to living evermore with Christ. Thrice happy are those who have received from heaven's Prince his gift of a life that death itself can never destroy. If we are among the number who have received him as our life, is it not our solemn obligation to introduce our Prince to those who are dead in their trespasses and sins? Does not the hymn say, "If Jesus has found you, tell others the story"?

A Glory That Transfigures You and Me

"Instead of the thorn shall come up the fir tree."
Isaiah 55:13.

Isaiah's prophecy of national and personal transformation in which thorns give way to fir trees is poetically emphasized in the lines of Julia Ward Howe's famous "Battle Hymn of the Republic":

> *In the beauty of the lilies, Christ was born, across the sea,*
> *With a glory in His bosom that transfigures you and me;*
> *As He died to make men holy, let us die to make men free.*

If Christ were born among the lilies, he died with thorns encircling his brow, thereby making possible for us the fir trees of holiness and freedom. Eastern farmers in Isaiah's day had to cultivate open land which, in the early spring, was covered with weeds and overrun with thorns so closely woven together that it was impossible to dig them up. Fire was the only remedy, and when kindled, weeds and thorns burned like paper. Thereafter, it was easy to dig up the old roots and prepare the land for the planting of fir trees.

The lesson all this enforces is that our hearts and minds are like the soil; they can be ruined by neglect or improved by cultivation. In his parable of the sower Jesus described how seed falling among thorns is quickly choked. If the seed is to bring forth fruit, it must fall into good or cultivated ground. It is said that soil grows weeds more readily than seeds, and that, according to an unknown source, "the soil is mother to the weeds, but she is only stepmother to the good seeds." The divine gardener knows how to destroy the weeds and thorns in the soil of the heart, enrich the soil, and cultivate useful trees. Those reclaimed by the Lord are referred to as stately trees. Planted by him, they are ever full of sap and honor him as trees of righteousness. May we allow this gardener to root up any thorn that may be in our heart and in its place plant a beneficial fir tree.

21

Great Minds—Such Should Govern

"Bethlehem . . . out of thee shall come a Governor."
Matthew 2:6.

In "The Prophetess" John Fletcher, quaint poet of the early seventeenth century, reminded us that:

'Tis virtue, and not birth that makes us noble:
Great actions speak great minds, and such should govern.

The nobility of his birth, his virtue, his great actions, and his great mind qualify Jesus to govern. Among his birth-cameos, none is more prophetic and suggestive than that of Governor, by which he is directly related to Israel and to a government having no end (Isa. 9:6–7).

The word Matthew used for *Governor* means one who goes first, leads the way, chief in war, and Jesus fulfills all these requirements of triumphant governorship. But as a Governor he is not a hard despot. He rules by love. Some governors who have risen from low positions become officious and unsympathetic. Not so with him who is ever our *fellow* and who sways our souls by his scars. Triumph is his because of the tree. And if we would govern in life, we too must go to a tree. Death of self leads to a diadem.

While universal government will yet be his, the present question of paramount importance is, Are we giving him more territory? Is his government of our life daily increasing? We can be certain that Satan will contest every inch of ground we yield to our heavenly Governor. But we have nothing to fear, for he is likewise our defender. Philip Massinger of the seventeenth century wrote in "The Bondman":

He that would govern others, first should be
The master of himself.

Great Heir of Fame

"Whom he hath appointed heir of all things." *Hebrews 1:2.*

In his "Epitaph on Shakespeare" John Milton wrote of the famous Bard as "Dear son of memory, great heir of fame." But is not the Savior a greater heir of fame? Paul described him as "the heir of God" (Rom. 8:17).

Jesus had this personal prerogative in mind when, in the parable of the householder, he said, "This is the heir; come, let us kill him" (Matt. 21:38), which they did at Calvary. But he rose again, ascended on high, and became the recipient as God's heir of a great domain in glory. To be an heir means that sooner or later one enters into possessions willed by someone. "God hath appointed Jesus heir of all things" (Heb. 1:2), and what vast possessions are to be his! Already he has received part of the treasure in his church. The possession of his full inheritance is still future when he will come into his own and every knee will bend before him.

The marvel of grace is that we are joint-heirs with him, that is, if we are the children of God through the regenerating ministry of the Holy Spirit. "If children, then heirs; heirs of God, and joint-heirs with Christ" (Rom. 8:16, 17). When the kingdoms of this world become his world kingdom, Jesus will make us co-rulers, for we are to reign with him. If only we could be more worthy of sharing all the coming honor and treasure of God's appointed heir and daily live as those who are joint-heirs with Christ! May he teach us how to possess our possessions here and now as heirs of salvation, the purchase of God.

At Their Hearts the Fire's Center

"They came to him from every quarter." *Mark 1:45.*

The verse from "I Think Continually of Those" by Stephen Spender, a modern poet, is worthy of attention:

> *I think continually of those who were truly great.*
> . . . .
> *The names of those who in their lives fought for life,*
> *Who wore at their hearts the fire's center.*

If we would be truly great in fighting the good fight of faith, Jesus must be in the fire center of our hearts. Longfellow would have us know that "every arrow that flies feels the attraction of earth." As arrows in the hands of the Almighty we must ever feel the attraction of Jesus to whom men came from every quarter. They found themselves drawn to him as filings to a magnet. Because of his unusual personality, unique teachings, and marvelous works, those in all walks of life were compelled to tread the pathway leading to his feet. All kinds of persons were drawn to him who is the center and circumference of all things.

And they are still coming to him from every quarter of the globe because there is none other to whom the needy of earth can go. He alone has the word of eternal life and is the unfailing source of all the best the heart craves. They are coming to him out of all nations, out of all conditions of life, and out of all ages, for young and old alike have found in him their heart's true center. The question is, Have we come to him from the quarter of our need and found in him your never-failing treasure, full with boundless stores of grace?

The Invincible Knights of God

"The people that do know their God shall be strong and
do exploits." *Daniel 11:32.*

Throughout the Bible God is found making a strong appeal to the heroic
in his own. He would have them function as his noble knights and, to
adapt Shakespeare's phrase in *I Henry IV*, never "usurp the sacred name
of knight." Quaint Chaucer could write of one who was "a very perfect,
gentle knight." Garibaldi, the Italian patriot, has been described as a
"gentle hero."

God calls us to action and summons us to aggressive service; as his
happy warriors we are not to be daunted by difficulties. The gospel is
brought to us in terms of battle—the sword, the shield, the armor, the
soldier, the enemy, the fight. It is God who teaches our fingers to war.
From the literature of courage the Bible furnishes, we have sufficient to
support the fighting spirit of our faith. As soldiers of the cross we must
manifest a militant spirit. We must dare to be a Daniel. Sir Walter Scott
felt that a fitting epitaph on "Marmion's lowly tomb" would be:

> *He died a gallant knight,*
> *With sword in hand, for England's right.*

It is thus that God's gallant knights should live and die defending
his right. As "every morning brings a noble chance," so every chance
should bring out "a noble knight." In these days of spiritual delusion,
abounding iniquity, and actions hostile to God and truth, we have need
to pray for more iron in our blood, more courage in our piety, more of
the bracing north in our personal witness. Tennyson's verse in *Idylls of
the King* provides us with a challenging example to follow:

> *And indeed he seems to me*
> *Scarce other than my own ideal knight,*
> *"Who reverenced his conscience as his king;*
> *Whose glory was, redressing human wrong;*
> *Who spake no slander, no, nor listened to it."*

The Red Gods Shall Call Us Out

"He shall honour the god of forces." Daniel 11:38.

Rudyard Kipling's expressive phrase "The red gods call us out and we must go" refers to the gods whose hands are red with the blood of those slain in war and are thus the gods of forces or of munitions about which Daniel wrote. The New American Standard Bible translates, "He will honour a god of fortresses, a god whom his fathers did not know . . . a foreign god." Antiochus, whose blasphemous pride he shared with Alexander the Great (Dan. 8:4, 11:3), called himself "King Antiochus, God Manifest." The god of fortresses he worshiped was probably Zeus for whom Antiochus built a temple near Antioch. This fearsome person, called "the little horn," is the forerunner of "the man of sin," the coming Antichrist who will magnify himself above every god.

World War II, the bloodiest war in all history, plunged the world into unparalleled misery because one man worshiped the god of munitions. Since then the reliance of nations upon such a red god has become more evident, and astronomical sums are being spent on nuclear bombs, other dreadful engines of destruction, and national defense. Although the Bible declares that no king can be saved by the multitude of a host or by his trust in tanks, planes, and bombs, the rulers of nations prefer to depend on their red gods rather than upon the God who with a breath destroyed 185,000 godless, God-defying Assyrians. Bless him. He is high over all.

Be a Star in Someone's Sky

"Shine . . . as the stars for ever and ever." *Daniel 12:3.*

Movie centers of the world speak of their top-ranking performers as *stars* and *starlets*. What a degradation of terms! The majority of those whose names are emblazoned as stars have no more real brilliance about them than a can of boot polish. Further, although advertised and applauded as stars, their appearance is but for a little. Many of them end up putting out their own light in suicidal death.

Star names quickly disappear from print, and new so-called stars appear. But Daniel would have us know that soul-winners are to shine as stars forever. Permanent brilliance is to be theirs. Having turned many to righteousness, they are to shine as the brightness of the firmament. Those who were wise followed a star to the feet of Jesus.

Are you a star in someone's sky? We often sing with Eliza Hewitt, "Will there be any stars, any stars in my crown?" Too many of us will face Jesus at reward day with a saved soul but a lost life—no souls to our credit. May yours be the honor of eternal radiance of the star that led many to Jesus who himself is to appear as the "Bright and Morning Star." He is indeed "Star of our might, and hope of every nation." Emerson urged us to "hitch our wagon to a star." If the wagon of our life is eternally hitched to him who is our "Star and Sun," then he in turn will endow us with all necessary wisdom to lighten the way of those lost in the darkness of sin and come to find in the Savior the one able to transform them into his marvelous light. A final word—we read of "wandering stars." God forbid that we should be in such a galaxy.

Thou Art Absolute Sole Lord

"A Saviour, who is Christ the Lord." *Luke 2:11.*

That spiritually quaint poet of the early seventeenth century, Richard Crashaw, in a hymn to St. Theresa of Avila wrote:

> *Love, thou art absolute sole Lord*
> *Of life and death.*

Since Jesus came as the personification of divine love and sacrificed his life for a lost world, he has every right to reign as our "absolute sole Lord." Luke's account of him suggests authority and dominion as Messiah and Lord accruing from his death at Calvary. Shortly after his ascension the apostles could preach that "God hath made that same Jesus . . . both Lord and Christ" (Acts 2:36). Once despised, he will yet reign as the "absolute sole Lord," as Lord of all. He is Lord of our life and the Lord of death, since "the keys of Death and Hell" dangle from his girdle.

Hudson Taylor, founder of the China Inland Mission, used to say that if Jesus is not "Lord of all, he is not Lord at all." We may believe him to be the Lord of hosts, able to deal with any or all circumstances and to carry out his will in spite of demons and people, yet we may not crown him as the sole Lord of our life. We have allowed other lords to have dominion over us and have failed to sanctify the Savior in our hearts as Lord. Life has been lived independently of him whose lordship ever makes for the spiritual enrichment of those who lovingly give him his rightful place of sovereignty. If we call him Lord, may we be found doing the things he says.

The Invisible Citadel

"My son, give Me thine heart." *Proverbs 23:26.*

Our heart is not something we wear on our sleeve for all and sundry to see, but, as Peter expresses it when referring to outward adornments, easily conspicuous "the hidden man of the heart" (I Peter 3:4). Yet, although unseen, like the covered mainspring of a watch, it is the most important part of our human mechanism. In his own captivating, Scottish style, Robert Burns wrote of the *heart* of man as being the part that makes him right or wrong. The marvel is that the One whose workmanship the heart is, asks for it to occupy as his throne from which to rule our whole life.

Having fashioned it by his power, God now wants to reign from it by his grace, for he knows that if he has the heart, he has all, for out of it are the issues of life. If the heart is God's undisputed habitation, then the outer life will be resplendent with his holiness. The secret of godlikeness is to commence each new day with a fresh surrender of our inner citadel to God to sanctify by his grace, engrave upon it his own image, and preserve by his power from the corrupt influences without that would change the heart into a stable of sin. Only the pure in heart is qualified to see God. Such a "vision splendid" is the privilege of all who seek to perfect holiness in the fear of the Lord. Was it not the Master himself who described himself as being "meek and lowly in heart," and that if we emulate his humility we too can find an inner peace and rest and nothing in a turbulent world can disturb or destroy (Matt. 11:28–30).

As Robert Burns says in his "Epistle to Davie":

> *The heart aye's the part aye*
> *That makes us right or wrong.*

Heaven's Matchless King

"Where is he that is born King?" *Matthew 2:2.*

In his religious masterpiece *Paradise Lost* John Milton graphically described those evil forces "warring in Heaven against Heaven's matchless King" who, being "matchless," conquers all his foes. The question of the wise men is of great import. *Born King!* It is very rare indeed for one of royal blood to be born a king. Born a prince, yes, but only becoming king when his father either abdicates or dies. But Jesus was *born* King, implying that he was a King before he was born. Paul could write of him as "the King eternal" (1 Tim. 1:17).

That Christ was a truer King than Herod who sought his life is evident from the capital *K* given to Jesus and the small *k* to the Roman ruler. All kings are small before our matchless King. The world has yet to see him as the King of kings. But strange insignia of royalty awaited the King born in Bethlehem. A stable was his palace; his courtiers, the lowly shepherds; his throne, a mother's knee; his robe, the swaddling clothes; his diadem, a crown of thorns.

Valiant knights said of King Arthur, "We never saw his like; there lives no greater leader." The glory of Arthur, however, pales into nothingness alongside the richer glory of Christ our King. It is thus we sing, "Hail Jesus, King of my days and nights." When he comes as King and ushers in his millennial reign, his kingdom will stretch from shore to shore. Is he King of our lives, exercising his sovereign rights over all we are and have? If so, then it will be evident to all we contact that being his children we resemble him as King (Judg. 8:18, 19). With loving obedience let us serve our King of glory.

Two Visitors from Heaven

"There talked with Jesus two men . . . Moses and Elijah."
Luke 9:30.

What a remarkable episode is the Gospel story of the manifestation of glory on Mt. Hermon! We could devote our meditation solely to the glorious transfiguration of Jesus when the deity within him sprang to the light of day and the three disciples were overawed as they beheld his glory. As Jesus prayed, the fashion of his countenance was changed, and prayer can secure for us a radiant transfiguration.

We are, however, concerned here with the two men who came down from heaven for the express purpose of having a talk with Jesus about his death at Jerusalem. On Mt. Nebo Moses was kissed to sleep by the angels, and God buried him in a secret grave—the only man to have had God as his undertaker! Elijah, however, never died, for like Enoch before him he was raptured, caught up in a whirlwind, to heaven. Yet both famous figures returned to earth and were immediately recognized by Peter, proving that they had not lost their identity and that they also were alive.

How consoling is the truth that our loved ones who departed in Christ are not mantled in a dreamless sleep but like Moses and Elijah are in full possession of their faculties with their gracious Lord who is "the God of the living." The bodies of the godly dead sleep but await a glorious resurrection. "I believe in the resurrection of the body." But the Christian dead themselves have been raised already and sit together with Christ. None can awaken what is awake or bring to life what never ceased to live. The appearance then of Moses and Elijah on the mount assures our hearts that those who leave us and whose bodies are left to lie like fallen trees, like the Lord they are with, are alive forevermore.

The Umpire Between Us

"Jesus the mediator of a better covenant." *Hebrews 12:24.*

The word Job uses for *daysman* is equivalent to the New Testament *mediator* and implies an *umpire* or a person chosen to decide a question. Job's lament (9:33), which the cross banishes, was:

> *There is no umpire between us,*
> *Who may lay his hand upon us both.*

This idea of mediation, of God dealing with the person, or the person with God, not directly, but through the interposition of another, is a prominent Scripture truth. The marvelous Epistle to the Hebrews has much to say about Jesus as the mediator or umpire between God and humankind, and surely there is no more expressive word of our Lord's sacrificial work on our behalf.

In these days of widespread industrial strife the word and office of mediator are often used. Capital and labor cannot agree; differences keep them apart, and an arbitrator is secured to bring both sides together to effect an amicable settlement. The Savior accomplished this by his cross. He laid his hand upon a holy and just God and a vile, lost sinner and reconciled them. Apart from his mediatorial work, we are helpless and homeless, and to reject him as the umpire means certain doom. "No man cometh unto the Father, *but by me*" (John 14:6).

Jesus is the only daysman between God and the person. Laying one hand on God and the other on the sinner, he makes them eternally one. The only way to an offended God then is through the pierced side of Jesus by which we can know what it is to be at peace with God. Would that sinners would heed his invitation, "Come, let us reason together. Though your sins are as scarlet, they will be white as snow" (Isa. 1:18).

The Hound of Heaven

"I will search Jerusalem with candles." *Zephaniah 1:12.*

It is not without reason that God was described by Francis Thompson as the Hound of Heaven, for unceasingly he tracks down sin to destroy it. Zephaniah, the prophet, was raised up to prophesy against the idolatrous practices and religious degeneracy of the people around him, and thus he declared that the Lord's search of their lives would be minute and thorough. He would search the corners of every life with a candle, even as the woman in the parable, with the aid of a candle, sought diligently for her lost piece of silver until she found it. David prayed for God to search the innermost recesses of his being. He wanted every nook and cranny scrutinized and so prayed, "Search me, know my thoughts . . . see if there be any wicked way *in me*" (Ps. 139:23, 24).

The Highlanders in Scotland use the more drastic word *ransack* for "search." "Ransack or turn me inside out, O God." Are we willing for the divine searcher, whose eyes are a flame of fire, to scan the very wounds shame would hide? Is it not folly to try to keep anything secret from him when he is the omniscient one? Does he not know us altogether? If the heavenly Hound is on our track, we have nothing to fear, for what the light of his candles reveal, his precious blood can cleanse. The primary object of his search is our sanctification. Are we prepared to pray, then, along with F. Bottome,

> *Search, till Thy fiery glance has cast*
> *Its holy light through all,*
> *And I, by grace, am brought at last,*
> *Before Thy face to fall.*

With Healing in His Wings

"He healed many who were ill with various diseases."
Mark 1:34.

During his public ministry Jesus gathered universal acclaim as the physician who never lost a case, and his miracles of healing established his deity and his mission as the sent one of God. "No man can do these miracles that thou doest, except God be with him" (John 3:2). His conquest over all manner of diseases, mental, physical, and demonic, proved him to be the Son of God with power and Lord over all. It must have been a great sight to watch him moving among the sick, afflicted, and distressed, relieving them of all affliction. An unidentified writer reflected:

Oh, in what divers pain they met!
Oh, with what joy they went away!

There were times, however, when the unbelief of people limited the manifestation of his miraculous power. He could have healed multitudes more, but unbelief, causing him to marvel, curbed his power to relieve the needy. Is it not blessed to know that his touch has still its ancient power? A remarkable saying of his was that his own would be able to accomplish greater works than even his miracles (John 14:12). It was indeed wonderful for him to impart physical healing, but when we lead a sin-sick soul to him and spiritual restoration is received, that is a greater miracle still. It was indeed wonderful to raise the dead, yet those quickened by his power died again. Our greater work is to bring those who are dead in their sin into the realization of life forevermore. Are *you* doing these greater works for your miracle-working Lord, whose touch has still its ancient power?

Give to a Gracious Message, a Host of Tongues

"Behold, I am going to send my messenger." *Malachi 3:1.*

The prophet Malachi mentions two messengers in the verse before us. "My messenger" refers to John the Baptist who came to declare the divine message of redemption and also to prepare the way for the redeemer himself who came as the "messenger of the covenant." His ministry as the heavenly messenger covers both of his returns, with special reference to the events following his coming. The function of a messenger is to deliver a message from one person to another. A post office messenger is only an intermediary and has nothing to do with the composition or content of the message, whether glad or sad. In *Antony and Cleopatra* Shakespeare declared that:

> *Though it be honest, it is never good*
> *To bring bad news. Give to a gracious message*
> *An host of tongues, but let ill tidings tell*
> *Themselves when they be felt.*

But a host of tongues in the Bible, including those of John the Baptist and of Jesus, sounded forth bad news as well as good. Jesus could say, "I have given them the words which thou gavest me." He did not originate the message he proclaimed, but receiving it from God, he declared it whether its content were heaven or hell. Would that all preachers were such messengers! Who and what is a messenger? He comes from the throne with a God-given message, and whether it pleases or pains, encourages or enrages, delivers it without apology or compromise. Are you a true messenger of the covenant of grace?

THE QUEEN

Blow trumpet, for the world is
white with May.

—Alfred Tennyson,
Idylls of the King

He Goes before Them and Commands Them All

"Behold, I have made him . . . a leader and commander."
Isaiah 55:4.

History provides us with thrilling stories of renowned commanders, like Napoleon, whose ability to lead and whose daring compelled multitudes to follow him, sometimes to disaster and death. In *Love's Labour's Lost* Shakespeare cited another notable leader and commander:

> *When in the world I liv'd, I was the world's commander;*
> *By east, west, north, and south I spread my conquering might;*
> *My scutcheon plain declares that I am Alisander.*

But in Jesus we have one given by God to command his people, and beside him the bravest and the best pale into insignificance. Think of the uncounted myriads who, at his command, left all and followed him even unto death! In the hour of his nation's travail Winston Churchill could offer nothing but "blood, sweat, and tears." And such a call electrified millions into sacrifice. With heaven's commander, sacrifice is ever the order of the day. All who follow him must take up a cross and deny themselves. There are many who drop out by the way. They find complete obedience to his commands too hard. For them there must be an easier round to travel. A picnic, not a battlefield, suits them better.

Our heavenly commander is incomparable in that he was the first to fall in the battle against Satan and his evil hordes. In his supreme victory all his followers are secure and by his death gather inspiration and strength to fight the good fight beneath his blood-red banner. An anonymous writer advised:

> *Thy Commander speaks: His word obey;*
> *So shall thy strength be as thy day.*

Continual Comfort in a Face

"I will not leave you comfortless: I will come to you."
John 14:18.

In the portion of this wonderful chapter where Jesus spoke of his coming ascension we find him promising, "I will pray the Father, and he shall give you another comforter" (John 14:16). The language Jesus used implies that while among his own he was their comforter with sweet comfort ever in his face, but since he was about to leave his followers, he would send another consoler to take his place. In the original the word *another* means two things. First, another of the *same* kind; second, another of a *different* kind. Which word do you think Jesus used? Why, the first—another of the same kind. Thus as he breathed his tender, last farewell, he bequeathed the Holy Spirit to them as one who would continue in his capacity as comforter, another like unto himself.

After Christ's ascension the disciples Jesus had left behind were found walking in "the comfort of the Spirit" (Acts 9:31). Scripture has much to say of the God of all comfort, as you will find by tracing the word *comfort* with the aid of a concordance. Paul would have us remember that God comforts us in all our tribulation that in turn we may comfort those who are in any trouble (2 Cor. 1:4).

As the result of our own heartaches, sorrows, and trials, have we been fashioned into missionaries of consolation to those who are now sitting where we sat? Are we being used to assure those who are passing through any dark valley that there is one known as the "Man of Sorrows" who can comfort their stricken hearts? Our own griefs will not be lost if they mold us into a Barnabas, a son of consolation, who refreshes the distressed and outworn saints along the way.

No Divinity Is Absent If Prudence Is Present

"Behold, my servant shall deal prudently." *Isaiah 52:13.*

As Isaiah was portraying Jesus, the coming Messiah, he certainly illustrated the proverb of the Roman poet Juvenal in the title above, for as
the divine servant, the virtue of *prudence* was always evident in his dealings with men. The prophet's portrait was fulfilled abundantly in the
carefulness, wisdom, and discretion of the incarnate one. Have you ever
meditated upon the prudence of Jesus? We think of Jesus' heroism and
willing self-sacrifice, and rightly so, but seldom think of him as one
exhibiting the attractive grace of prudence. The word *prudent* as used
by Isaiah is two-sided, carrying the ideas of prudence and prosperity.
He shall deal prudently, so that prosperity shall be the result. Often
prudence on our part fails, but the Master's ever succeeded and conquered hearts by sagacity.

Paul spoke of Jesus abounding "in all wisdom and prudence." Thus
the apostle thought of Jesus' life as the manifestation of godlike
prudence. Cunning men sought to kill him before his time, but he knew
how to evade a premature death. Jesus prized life, not excessively, but
moderately, and his dealings with all men and women were ever prudent.
With adroitness he could meet all questions and face all difficult situa-
tions with an inborn discreteness. As servants of the Lord, have we
learned that prudence is essential to ultimate and permanent results in
his service? His prudence was not the brand of many so-called prudent
people, which is but the instinct of self-preservation acutely developed.
His self-sacrifice was the highest prudence—an example we must
emulate.

His Identity Presses upon Me

"But he could not be hid." *Mark 7:24.*

The New American Standard Bible translates Mark's item in his biography of Jesus as "when He had entered a house, He wanted no one to know *of it*, yet He could not escape notice." What an ageless truth there is in this historical fact! How could a personality like his be hid? As Matthew Henry commented, "A candle may be put under a bushel, the sun cannot." Did he not come as "*the* Light of the world," and was it not therefore impossible to hide such a glorious Orbit? A potent personality cannot be inconspicuous, and thus the solar presence of the Lord irradiated every region in which it tarried. He was the ever-evident Christ.

Lesser figures in Scripture may be shrouded in obscurity, but the glory of such an orb as Christ must attest himself everywhere. "He could not escape notice." It is affirmed that he hides himself and his purposes from us. "Verily, Thou art a God that hideth Thyself" (Isa. 45:15). He is certainly hid from the lost who have been blinded by the god of this world. None are so blind as those who won't see.

But can we who know him as the revealed one say that ours is the Christlike life revealing him to others? In a consecrated life he cannot be hid. A truly surrendered life forces Christ upon the gaze of the world. If we adorn his teachings in all things, then ours will be the witness showing forth his beauty. The perfume of holiness cannot be hid. *We* may escape notice, but that matters nothing so long as men see Jesus. "His identity," to quote and adapt John Keats, "presses upon me," and through me upon others.

Where Ignorance Is Bliss

"Moses wist not that the skin of his face shone while he talked with him." *Exodus 34:29.*

We cannot altogether agree with Christopher Marlowe that "there is no sin but ignorance." Rather do we believe as Thomas Gray of the eighteenth century expressed it in "Prospect of Eton College" "Where ignorance is bliss, 'Tis folly to be wise." In the chapter before us we find Moses, of "the shining face," miraculously sustained for forty days on the mount, then returning to earth with the best treasure in his hands, the two tables of the law, and adorned with the best beauty, for the skin of his face shone. Thus he carried the credential of his commission in his very countenance. Moses was oblivious of his transfigured face, and as Alexander Smellie, early twentieth-century Scottish minister, expressed it, "That is truest sainthood that never dreams of the beauty with which it is invested. Any self-consciousness detracts from the graciousness of a devout character, and lowers the disciple to lower levels."

The facial radiance of Moses was the effect of his sight of God, and when we have been on the mount with him, our light should shine before men as they take knowledge of us that we have been with Jesus. A devoted son wrote of his mother, "I read her face as one who reads a true and holy book." It is thus we read the supreme face of Jesus and how those around should read our faces as those who walk in the light with him.

Moses was ignorant of his shining face, and whatever beauty God puts upon us should fill us with a humble sense of our own unworthiness and cause us to forget that which makes our faces shine. Moses put a veil upon his face when he became conscious it shone. But when he went before the Lord, he put off the veil, and with open face he beheld the glory of the Lord. May we be saved from the fatal ignorance of Samson who did not know that the Lord had departed from him.

Closer Is He Than Breathing

"The Lord is near." *Philippians 4:5.*

An old divine said of Paul's pregnant phrase: "It is even more compacted as Paul uttered it. What he literally said was—*The Lord near.* Three words! No verb was used, for none was needed. It is abrupt to the point of dramatism. It is a bolt of benediction."

Is it not comforting to know that Jesus is ever accessible and available and that he is not far removed from any one of us? "Closer is he than breathing, and nearer than hands and feet," Tennyson reminded us in "The Higher Pantheism." Through the darkest night and over the roughest road he is near as a friend sticking closer than a brother. How different life would be if only we could realize his presence at all times and under all circumstances! May grace be ours to rest in his abiding nearness.

Others, so near and dear to us, have left us and are no longer at hand to soothe and sympathize, but Jesus is ever at our side, even within our heart to undertake for us under all circumstances. While it is true that ills have no weight and tears no bitterness when Jesus is at hand to bless, we can make another application of Paul's affirmation. The chaotic condition of the world would seem to indicate that the return of the Lord is at hand. He is certainly nearer his second coming than when we first believed. Here is the only hope for a broken world: "The Lord is near." In the gloom of this midnight hour, his trumpet may sound and his glory blaze upon us. Can we say that we are ready to hail him? Are we living near to him who is ever near us? If so, we shall not be surprised when he appears for the final installment of our redemption.

Comparisons Are Odorous

"What is your beloved more than another beloved?"
Song of Solomon 5:9.

There are occasions when comparisons are *odious* and not *odorous*, as Shakespeare said many comparisons are. There is a fragrancy about Solomon's figure of the bride extolling her lover above all other lovers. To her he was dazzling and ruddy and outstanding among ten thousands who also knew how to love. To the spiritual mind Solomon's Song is strikingly typical of the union existing between Christ and his church. As our beloved, he is beyond the best of earth altogether. He is incomparable, peerless, without an equal.

Often Jesus is compared with great religious leaders, but he is beyond compare. But does he ravish our hearts as he ought to? Is he precious beyond all preciousness, even as the one whose price is above rubies? The bride in Solomon's Idyll was so captivated by her beloved that she sang his praises everywhere. She was so intoxicated with love for him that she could not be silent as to his adorable person and virtues. Is this our attitude toward him who is the fairest of all the earth besides? Silence where his worth is concerned is treachery. May grace be ours to declare in glad tones our heavenly beloved's charms! If we deem him "the chiefest among ten thousand" and the one "altogether lovely," then let our lips publish his love and loveliness abroad so that others can see his beauty and come to desire him. Charles W. Fry shared his discovery:

> *I have found a friend in Jesus, he's everything to me,*
> *He's the fairest of ten thousand to my soul;*
> *The Lily of the Valley, in him alone I see*
> *All I need to cleanse and make me fully whole.*

Here Is My Throne

"Christ in you, the hope of glory." *Colossians 1:27.*

The root of Christ's teaching in the Gospels reaches a rich fruitage in the Epistles. He often spoke to his own about being *in* them, and it was given to Paul fully to expound the glorious truth of Christ's indwelling our hearts by faith (Eph. 3:17). Then for the Colossians was the mystic truth, *Christ in you.* What a precious gem this is from the casket of pearls found in the first chapter of this Christ-exalting epistle! Spurgeon said of verse 27, "The words read like a whole body of divinity condensed in a line."

At Calvary it was Christ *for* us, but since Pentecost it is Christ *in* us by his Spirit. He died for us that he might be in us. Such then is the mystery of our faith that although Christ is in heaven, throned in glory everlasting, he yet indwells you and me. Thus he has two thrones: one above, glorious beyond compare; the other, a saved and trustful heart. Paul reminded us that Christ dwells in our heart *by faith*—the little unimposing door by which he enters human personalities.

Further, he himself declared, "Greater is he that is in you than he that is in the world," and being within, he is the sanctifying principle of life. Indwelling us, he ever seeks to transform us into his image. Then is not his indwelling the hope of the glorious life to come? His presence within us is the basis of "that blessed hope," about which Paul reminded Titus. Does not the constant remembrance of indwelling deity keep such a hope of glory vivid and vital in our present life? May we know him increasingly both as the indweller and as the friend sticking closer than a brother.

To Err Is Human, to Forgive, Divine

"Thy sins are forgiven thee." *Luke 5:20.*

Jesus preached and practiced forgiveness. He urged his disciples to forgive until seventy times seven and to forgive their enemies. At Calvary he prayed God to forgive his murderers. Christ's forgiveness of the palsied man raised the ire of the unforgiving Pharisees. Condemning Christ with blasphemy, they said, "Who can forgive sins, but God alone?" This was true. God alone can forgive. What they forgot, however, was that God was in Christ, who was therefore qualified to forgive. Further, the revelation is that when he forgives he forgets, remembering our sins no more against us.

Are we forgiven? Have we proved that there is forgiveness with him that he may be feared? How blessed we are if "ransomed, healed, restored, forgiven"! And if God, for Christ's sake, has forgiven us, then it is our responsibility to emulate the divine example and be found "tenderhearted, forgiving one another." On the basis of a divinely bestowed forgiveness we must manifest the Christlike virtue toward others.

Is there someone you should forgive, but is your attitude one of reluctance? How often we hear one say, "I can never forgive them for what they have done." How would we fare if this were God's attitude toward us who have sinned exceedingly? We manifest the virtue of divinity when we forgive, even as we have been forgiven by God in virtue of Calvary. Have we personally experienced the blessedness of the man whose sin has been forgiven? Then our obligation is to manifest such a divine action in dealing with others.

His Mind, His Kingdom, His Will Is Law

"Lord, if thou wilt . . . I will: be thou clean." Luke 5:12, 13.

Can you not hear the chiming of wedding bells in the miracle Jesus performed the day he cleansed the leper of his foul disease? The marriage vows read, "Wilt thou take this man?" and the answer is, "I will." The diseased man said to Jesus, "If thou wilt?" and Jesus replied, "I will." Truly a marriage took place as the two met face-to-face, for the Lord and the one-time leper became one.

No one can read the Gospels without being impressed with Christ's willingness to heal and cleanse, to forgive and save. At all times he was ready and willing to relieve the distressed; in fact, he was more willing to bless than the needy were to be blessed. Did he not have to say, "Ye will not come to me, that ye might have life" (John 5:40)?

Jesus is not willing that any should perish, but, alas, multitudes willingly go to hell. He waits to heal all of their moral leprosy, but he cannot exercise his power to cleanse and deliver unless his will and the human will harmonize. A sinner is halfway saved when he is willing for Jesus to say to him, "Be thou clean!" If a man wills to know Jesus' will, he comes to experience all the healer can accomplish in his heart and life. We learn from a hymn translated by John Mason Neale:

> *If I ask Him to receive me*
>   *Will He say me, Nay?*
> *Not till Earth, and not till Heaven*
>   *Pass away.*

The Kingly Crowned Head

"The first man is of the earth, earthy: the second man is the Lord from heaven." *1 Corinthians 15:47.*

In many ways Christ, our federal head, is a contrasting type of Adam. As the first man, Adam was fashioned out of dust; Jesus was conceived by the Holy Spirit. Adam was created innocent; Jesus came as the holy, perfect one. Adam became a sinner; Jesus knew no sin. Through Adam we have physical life; through Christ we have life forevermore. Adam was of the earth; Jesus came from heaven. In Adam we bear the image of earthly things; in Jesus we bear the image of heavenly things. Adam was the natural head of the human race; Jesus is the head of a new creation (Luke 3:38; Rom. 5:14). In Adam we die; in Jesus we are made alive. By his sin Adam brought ruin to mankind; by his obedience Jesus brings blessing to all who, although the sinning sons of Adam's race, receive him as savior. In a garden Adam succumbed to the wiles of Satan; in another garden Jesus overcame the enemy of humankind. The first Adam derived his life from another; Jesus came as the life and as the life-giving spirit, or as the fountain of life, able to impart life to others, whether physical, spiritual, or eternal.

As the whole of humanity can be separated under two heads, namely, Adam or Jesus, in which are you to be found? You must be in one or the other, either in sin or in grace, either saved from the guilt and penalty of sin or lost in sin and in danger of being lost eternally. Is Christ your head, directing all that concerns your life? If found in him, then walking in the light with him counteracts the wiles of the old Adamic nature.

Powerful Preacher and Tenderest Teacher

"From that time Jesus began to preach." *Matthew 4:17*.

Although it was Father O'Flynn of "ould Donegal" that the poet Augustus P. Gardner had in mind as the "powerful preacher," I recall the description used of a still more powerful preacher. Now and again some eloquent pulpiteer, like Charles H. Spurgeon, is referred to as "a prince of preachers." But there has only been one princely preacher, and there will never be his like again. "Never man spake like this man" (John 7:46). If only we could have listened to the discourses that made him the greatest preacher the world has ever known. As the master preacher he knew how to "open his mouth" (Matt. 5:2). He opened it because he knew what to preach about, and he preached it simply, clearly, and distinctly. Beautiful indeed were his feet as he journeyed here and there preaching peace.

To Jonah came the command, "Preach the preaching that I bid thee," and Jesus appeared as a God-sent, Spirit-inspired preacher preaching nothing but a God-given message. "I have given unto them the words which thou gavest me" (John 17:8). That he practiced what he preached is evident from a study of the Gospels. With him, lips and life were in complete harmony. His influence as a preacher did not bring high, bestowed honors but a cross of agony and shame. And now the kind of preaching he always blesses is the preaching of that cross as the only remedy for sin. The world sadly needs more preaching that will cause sinners to flee to Jesus from the wrath to come.

Fairest of All the Earth Beside

"He is altogether lovely." *Song of Solomon 5:16.*

We read that Saul and Jonathan were lovely and pleasant in their lives, but Jesus is preeminent among men for his loveliness and pleasantness. Are you not amazed as you meditate upon the extent and variety of descriptions and designations, definite and implied, setting forth the excellencies of God's beloved Son? And it takes them all to set forth his perfections, including his tender relation with his own and as the center of God's counsels. Those who are taught of the Spirit cannot fail to see Jesus in Solomon's matchless Song. There are so many naturally beautiful things in the world, and because he fashioned them all, how lovely he must be. His beauty must be beyond compare. Not only is he lovely in form and feature, but in every word and wish. Everything about him bears the imprint of his exquisite attractiveness. No wonder Zechariah cried, "How great is thy beauty!" (Zech. 9:17).

Can we say that the beauty of the Lord is upon us and that we are sharing his loveliness? Whether we have beauty of countenance or not makes little difference. Behind the plainest-looking face may be one of the loveliest of characters because of the indwelling of him who is "altogether lovely." Beholding the beauty of the Lord should result in the beauty of holiness in your life and mine. A proverb has it, "Handsome is as handsome does." We petition with Mrs. H. Bradley:

> *I ask this gift of Thee,*
> *A life all lily-fair,*
> *And fragrant as the place*
> *Where seraphs are.*

In Goodly Colors Gloriously Arrayed

"Blue, and purple, and scarlet, and fine linen." *Exodus 25:4.*

Dear old Edmund Spenser of the sixteenth century had all sorts of spring flowers in mind when he conceived the line in the above title. I like to use it to describe the beautiful colors employed in the tabernacle that Moses set up in the wilderness. Although the tents in which the Israelites lived were ordinary and commonplace, the sanctuary in the midst of them was resplendent with its scarlet roof, golden furniture, and gay-colored curtains. That God is a lover of the artistic is proven, not only by the blue, scarlet, white, and purple used in the tablernacle, but in the gorgeous, unmatched colors of the rainbow—his pledge that he will not flood the earth again.

The costly and beautiful tabernacle occupies a most important place in the story of redemption, hence, the space devoted to it in Scripture. At most, Moses devoted only two chapters to the creation of the world; but his record of the tabernacle and the consecration of its priests spread itself into thirteen chapters.

The royal colors mentioned are symbolic. *Blue* is the color of the sky and suggests heavenly peace—"as it were the body of heaven in his clearness" (Exod. 24:10). The deep blue of the firmament leads us to think of the sweet peace of God, the most real and precious of blessings. *Purple* is the royal and imperial color and carries first the thought of sovereignty, then of grace, grace being the most attractive form in which sovereignty manifests itself.

Scarlet is both the sin and sacrifice color. Though our sins are as scarlet, the sacrifice at Calvary provides a full cleansing and deliverance. *White* consists of the union of the seven prismatic colors forming the rainbow, and in the tabernacle white was the background of all, the ground on which the lovely hues were wrought. White is the color of holiness and purity, and in heaven the bride of the lamb will be arrayed in fine linen, clean and white. Blue, purple, and scarlet are ours in the "grace, mercy, and peace" from God; and white is our purity of heart and life in response to all we have from God.

A Traveler between Life and Death

"A certain householder . . . went into a far country."
Matthew 21:33.

The traveler between life and death that Wordsworth depicted in "She Was a Phantom of Delight" was a virgin with "reason firm, the temperate will, . . . a perfect Woman, nobly planned." But in his Olivet discourse, under the guise of a householder making all arrangements about his possessions before traveling into a far country, Jesus painted a precious portrait of himself. In this parable, so full of spiritual teaching, Jesus described his departure from the earth and the committal of responsibilities to his servants he was to leave behind. At his ascension he was the glorified man traveling from a world where death reigned into the far country of heaven with its life, eternal in nature.

During his absence he expects his own to be faithful in their stewardship. With the coming of his Spirit at Pentacost, gifts were imparted for service, some being more gifted than others. As all of us have a gift of some sort or another, the question is, Are we using our Christ-bestowed talents to the full? During the absence of the traveling man, are we trading with and multiplying our talents?

Having taken his journey, he left us behind to take his goods and distribute them among the needy. He does not expect five talents more from the one who has only two talents. Whether we have five, two, or one makes little difference. Reward can only be ours when he returns from the far country if we have used to the limit what he gave us to serve him with. What folly it was for the man with the one talent to bury it in a handkerchief. He should have used to it wipe the sweat from his brow as he used his talent unceasingly.

None Invincible As They

"If God be for us, who can be against us?" *Romans 8:31.*

Cowper was poetically describing the forces of the British warrior queen, Boadicea, as they faced Caesar's proud legions, when he wrote, "None invincible as they." But Paul, who also knew something of the might and cruelty of Rome, assured us that the soldiers of the heavenly warrior King have a far greater invincibility than that experienced by Boadicea's brave fighters. Hence the apostle's challenge, "If [or *since*] God is for us, who can be against us?" (Rom. 8:31). Satan and a godless world will ever be lined up against the saints, but in spite of all assaults they are invincible, emerging from the conflict more than conquerors. From the Psalms Paul gathered inspiration to encourage believers to stand firm. "The Lord is for me, I will not fear; What can man do unto me?" (Ps. 118:6).

If there is no suggestion of doubt here, we should read the verse, "Since God be for us." Is not his name *Emmanuel*—God with us? Therefore, all the perfections of his nature are arrayed for the defense and safety of those fighting the good fight of faith. God is committed by his covenant, his oath, and his promise to support and sustain us and to bring us through to victory. Our cause is his. Thus he is opposed to all who are against us and has pledged to deliver us in six contests and not to forsake us in the seventh.

Amid all opposition to our faithful witness let us take fresh heart, for our ally is the Lord God omnipotent who is able to clothe us with invincibility. None can prevail over us, for he that is in us is greater than satanic foes in the world. Because God is with and for us, we can overcome the world, conquer death, and eternally inherit glory. God is ours, and we are God's. Why then should anything or anybody alarm or terrify us?

Let Gentleness My Strong Enforcement Be

"Thy gentleness hath made me great." *Psalm 18:35.*

The word *gentleness* is translated in many ways. The Book of Common Prayer has it, *"Thy loving correction has made me great."* Our developing character owes much to divine correction. "Thy *goodness* hath made me great." David often gratefully ascribed all his greatness, not to his own goodness, but to the unfailing goodness of God. Another reading puts it, "Thy *providence,*" and divine providence is nothing more than goodness in action. "Goodness is the bud of which Providence is the flower." Some render it, "Thy humility hath made me great" or "Thy condescension hath made me great!" Spurgeon said, "We are so little, that if God should manifest His greatness without condescension, we should be trampled under His feet; but God, who must stoop to view the skies, and bow to see what angels do, turns His eye yet lower, and looks to the lowly and contrite, and makes them great." The Chaldean clay tablet reads, "Thy word hath increased me." But the virtue of gentleness—the Roman emperor Aurelius called it *invincible*—is a prominent feature of deity. Shakespeare wrote in *As You Like It*:

> ... *Your gentleness shall force*
> *More than your force move us to gentleness.*

In childhood days we were taught to sing, "Gentle Jesus, meek and mild," and marvelous has our experience been of his gentleness. How gentle he has been in his corrections, his forbearance, his instruction, and his patience! As we meditate upon such a theme as his gentle treatment of us, may gratitude be awakened, love quickened, and humility deepened. It is only thus that spiritual greatness can become ours. St. Aidian would have us remember that God "gently deals with souls untaught." May we ever be found beseeching others by the gentleness of God.

He Sung of God—the Mighty Source

"Bring them hither to me." *Matthew 14:18.*

Because the Son of God was "the hidden source of every precious thing," he knew he could feed the starving, fainting multitude around him. Christopher Smart, godly poet of the eighteenth century, praised the psalmist in "A Song to David":

> *He sung of God—the mighty source*
> *Of all things—the stupendous force.*
> *On which all strength depends.*

In the command of Jesus, "Bring them to me," there was power to perform miracles with the little we may have to give him. One of our hymns speaks of him as "Thou source of all our store" and as "The source of all our bliss." We can bring the poor and needful and sinful to him because he alone has the resources to relieve them.

Have we learned the secret of bringing everything to him—our homes, our children, our business obligations? *Bring them to me!* Are trials, sorrows, heartaches, disappointments, and losses ours? Jesus, the source of sympathetic tears, is saying, Bring them to me, and my provision will sweeten your bitter cup. Have you a particular, peculiar problem or trouble facing you just now? Then close your eyes for a moment and hear Jesus say, "Bring it hither to me." As you do, yours will be assurance that as all things are possible to him he will give you grace to surmount your trial and joy in God. An unknown author wrote:

> *How sweet to be allow'd to call*
> *The God whom heaven adores my Friend,*
> *To tell my thoughts, to tell Him all;*
> *And then to know my prayers ascend.*

The Crown of Sovereignty

"Thy God reigneth." *Isaiah 52:7.*

With united voice Scripture acclaims the sovereignty of him who is the almighty one. As the Lord God omnipotent he is worthy to wear the crown of sovereignty, for his supremacy in every realm cannot be disputed. He sits upon the throne of the universe he created and can use the forces of nature as he deems best. His will as the sovereign Lord cannot be frustrated. No one and nothing can frustrate the accomplishment of his designs. All events are under his control as the superintendent of all things. In these days of international and national crises and upheavals, those of us who love God should encourage our hearts in his supremacy. Laws may be proposed contrary to his will, but he can dispose of them. He rules and overrules. None can stay his hand or say to him, What doest thou?

He reigns, not as a tyrant lord, but as our heavenly Father, seeking to secure our well-being and his glory. He reigns to crush his foes and convert them into his friends. Is this not the sublime truth that should calm and compose our minds at all times—my God reigneth? Amid crumbling empires, look up and see him on his throne as King forever and rejoice. His sovereignty ensures your safety, happiness, and deliverance.

Are the reins of the government of your life in his hands? Does he reign without a rival in your heart? If so, then you will have no doubt as to his universal dominion and supremacy both now and in the future. Sir Robert Grant could write:

> O worship the King, all glorious above,
> And gratefully sing His wonderful love.

Knit Together in One Fellowship

"Whether we be afflicted, it is for your consolation."
2 Corinthians 1:6.

A portion of the collect for All Saints' Day in the Book of Common Prayer reads, "Who hast knit together thine elect in one communion and fellowship, in the mystical body of Thy Son." One aspect of this fellowship of kindred minds concerns pain and comfort, as the chapter from which our text is taken clearly proves. This is preeminently the Comfort Chapter of the New Testament. Paul had had some dark experiences, including an affliction when he would have died had it not been for God's intervention. But through all his suffering the apostle experienced the comfort of God and was brought to see that his severe trials and the unfailing consolation of God through them all were but a preparation for his ministry of comforting others.

Often God afflicts us first and then heals and consoles us because he wishes to fashion us into missionaries of comfort among those in any trouble. Our own sorrows and trials are not squandered or lost when they mold us into sons and daughters of consolation. Alexander Smellie reminded us that "there are many around me on whom griefs like my own are laid; and who upholds and strengthens them so well as one who has been in the wilderness of desolation and the gloomy Valley of Death's Shade before them?"

If we have never known heartbreak, we are not qualified to assure the brokenhearted of reality of divine comfort. A world of pain and grief is a grim reality, and there are secrets we could never learn unless we become personally acquainted with the trials and afflictions of those around. One of these secrets is the presence of the divine comforter in our trouble, resulting in the ability to comfort others as we ourselves were comforted of God.

I Tremble for My Country

"His heart trembled for the ark of God." *1 Samuel 4:13.*

Thomas Jefferson, the American president who died in 1826, said, "Indeed I tremble for my country when I reflect that God is just." Aging Eli knew that God was just and trembled for his country as the ark was being taken by godless hands. The prophet shuddered to think what it would mean for Israel if the ark were lost to the nation. Israel's glory would depart, for the ark had been at once the symbol and pledge of the presence of Jehovah in the midst of his people—a presence to which they owed everything. Behind Eli's trembling of heart was a smitten conscience, for he had permitted flagrant abuses in its holy precincts and had allowed the ark to go from its holy and peaceable habitation out to the clamor and carnage of the battlefield. Yet Eli dearly loved the ark, which acted as a magnet drawing the warmth and emotion of his soul.

Christ is the Ark of the Covenant, and if all he represents as the mercy seat departs, we have a creed with life and a temple without the presence of the Lord. Eli felt he could not live if the ark were disgraced or banished. In fact, at its removal he died. Is this our estimate of Christ in spite of the wounds we have inflicted upon him?

When Principal Fulloch, conservative theologian, was dying in Torquay, his wife, Jeanie, was at their home in St. Andrews. As he died, he kept uttering a plaintive cry, unconscious of what he was saying but conscious of the one earthly thing he wanted—*Jeanie! Jeanie!* As he went down into the valley, his whole being called for her who had been his constant companion. Can we say that this is our longing when Christ our ark seems removed? *Jesus, Jesus, leave me not.* Bless him, we have no need to tremble, for nothing can separate us from him!

A Victorious Name

"The breaker is come up before them." *Micah 2:13.*

Of the many names and titles of the Lord, *breaker* is one of the most forceful. Micah, stirred by the injustice and oppression associated with the house of Jacob, envisaged a decisive deliverance for the people. As Charles John Ellicott, late eighteenth-century bishop of Gloucester, commented, "The Breaker shall go before them as their Saviour and Deliverer, yea, even Jehovah at their head. . . . This Breaker is, by confession of the Jews, the title of the Messiah. A saying of one of their famous Rabbis reads—'the explanation from above as Messiah, as it is written, *The Breaker is come up from before them.'* "

He is a mighty breaker, able to break down all opposition and clear a road out of all captivity. By his death and resurrection Jesus broke down and destroyed the forces of darkness and was victorious over every foe. As those delivered from the penalty and thralldom of sin, we do not march on *to* victory but *from* it, for the great enemy was overcome at Calvary. By faith we appropriate his triumph as ours. With Samuel Medley we

> *Sing the dear Saviour's glorious fame,*
> *Who bears* The Breaker's *wondrous name;*
> *Sweet name, and it becomes Him well,*
> *Who breaks down sin, guilt, death, and hell.*

The Lord is able to break in pieces all oppressors and go before his own as their victorious protector. May we take fresh heart from the fact that all our enemies were conquered beforehand and the prey taken from the mighty. Through the conquest of the cross, satanic foes, bent on hurting us, have had their weapons severely blunted. The old serpent would still try to destroy us, but his fangs have been extracted. As the roaring lion, his teeth have been broken. So let us praise our blessed *breaker.*

A Happy Issue out of All Their Afflictions

"In their affliction they seek me early." Hosea 5:15.

In the Book of Common Prayer is a petition for those in "any ways afflicted, or distressed, in mind, body, or estate." It pleads that for them there may be "a happy issue out of all their afflictions." Hosea described how the people could find a happy issue out of their national affliction, namely, by seeking the Lord, not only *early* or at once, but earnestly. "In their affliction they will earnestly seek me." Hosea said that God's withdrawal from his people was not absolute and final but was a method intended to produce a result which could make his return possible. And when his people sought him earnestly, God returned to them.

Often God uses our adversities and afflictions as the means to bring us nearer himself—always a happy issue! Charles H. Spurgeon said that afflictions are frequently "like fierce dogs to worry wanderers back to the fold." If we are rich and increased with goods and boasting like David, "In my prosperity . . . I shall never be moved" (Ps. 30:6), God often applies the rod, and what we have treasured disappears. Our carnal security vanishes, and, stripped of our pride, we earnestly seek the Lord. Then our emptiness is sanctified to the enrichment of our soul. In abject poverty the prodigal son said, "I will arise, and go unto my father." If we are heirs of affliction, as he rebukes us, let us recognize that it is a loving hand that chastens us and a loving heart that forgives us. The happy issue out of all afflictions is embodied for us in the words of the hymn by Elizabeth P. Prentiss:

> *Let sorrow do its work, Come grief and pain;*
> *Sweet are thy messengers, Sweet their refrain,*
> *When they can sing with me,—More love, O Christ, to thee,*
> *More love to thee!*

That Man's Silence Is Wonderful to Listen To

"But he answered her not a word." *Matthew 15:23.*

Thomas Hardy in *Under the Greenwood Tree*, described a character thus:

> *Silent? Ah, he is silent! He can keep silence well.*
> *That man's silence is wonderful to listen to.*

Over sixty years ago Percy Ainsworth left the church a precious heritage in his volume *The Silences of Jesus*, in which he makes us feel that it is wonderful to listen to the silences of the Master.

The silence that greeted the heartcry of the woman of Canaan for the healing of her sick daughter is called the "silence of love." This distressed soul had come a long way and had crossed the strong barrier of race when, as a Gentile, she made a request of a Jew. But she thought of Jesus more as a great healer and presented a simple plea, "Have mercy upon me, O Lord, thou Son of David; my daughter is grievously vexed with a devil" (Matt. 15:22). She expected an immediate reply, "but he answered her not a word." His silence was sympathetic and was designed to bring the distressed woman nearer the heart of infinite love and pity. Her second cry and answer to the refusal of Jesus brought forth his commendation, "O woman, great is thy faith: be it unto thee even as thou wilt" (Matt. 15:28).

Are there not times in our experience when, in spite of our pleading, heaven is silent? It is said that that great man of faith, George Muller, prayed for fifty years for the salvation of a friend before God answered his plea. God's silences do not mean denials. His silence is the richest test of our faith, for we have the assurance that if our requests are according to his will he must answer us. Another silence wonderful to listen to was his own when before his crucifiers he was dumb and opened not his mouth. By his silence he conclusively proved himself the true lamb of God. In the silence of our own hearts may we ever hear the voice of his love.

A Pleasant Shade, a Grove of Myrtles Made

"Instead of the brier shall come up the myrtle tree."
Isaiah 55:13.

Isaiah is conspicuous among the sacred writers in his love of, and unique ability to use, natural objects to symbolize spiritual truths. Briers have no beauty, yield no fragrance, and bear no fruit. They only cumber the ground and occupy soil well able to produce something more beneficial. Briers are, therefore, symbolic of all that is worthless and mischievous in the world and must be got rid of so that a wilderness can be turned into a garden. Myrtles, however, provide "a pleasant shade," as the fifteenth-century poet Richard Barnfield reminded us.

Looked upon as emblems of youth and loveliness, myrtles were deemed sacred by the ancients. They were used in all joyous festivals, especially those in honor of Venus. The bark of myrtles was used for tanning. The berries and leaves provided medicine, wine, and oil and thus remain as types of all that is pure, fragrant, and serviceable in the world. Changing briers for myrtles is a change for the better; and our age is in great need of the destruction of briers and the planting of myrtles.

History is laden with stories of courageous men who have uprooted briers and planted myrtles. In the days of William Wilberforce slavery was an ugly, cruel brier that died very hard, but self-denying patriots like Wilberforce and Abraham Lincoln labored unceasingly to expose the horrors of the slave trade. They lived to see the day when the brier of slavery was killed and the myrtle of freedom planted in its place. Godly souls, like John Bunyan, believed that persons should worship God in their own way and according to the dictates of their heart and consequently suffered torture, imprisonment, and even martyrdom for the sake of religious liberty. They succeeded in uprooting the brier of religious persecution and planting the myrtle tree of religious freedom. In the narrower world of our own hearts we must cast out the briers of disobedience, pride, selfishness, and sin and substitute the myrtles of obedience, humility, love, and holiness.

Watch Your Step

"Walk circumspectly, not as fools, but as wise."
Ephesians 5:15.

What an engaging term Paul used in his description of the walk and warfare of the believer! *Circumspect* means wary, taking everything into account, exercising caution. The Revised Version expresses the verse, "Look therefore carefully how ye walk, not as unwise but as the wise." We are to walk accurately, looking around, watchful on every side. As those redeemed by the precious blood of Jesus, we must be strict about our character and check up on our daily living with the deliberate purpose of correcting wrong decisions taken and of being self-controlled in every habit. Strictest consistency in common things is obligatory, for we are taught to avoid every appearance of evil. Only thus can we buy up every opportunity of doing good.

Surrounded as we are by the wiles of the Devil, we have to be careful of every step. In *Julius Caesar* Shakespeare wrote:

> *It is the bright day that brings forth the adder,*
> *And that craves wary walking.*

We live in a hostile, godless world surrounded by manifold temptations. Our heart is deceitful above all things and desperately wicked, and unless we keep close to Jesus, we cannot be victorious as we walk in the midst of snares. Honoring him in every phase of life should be our constant aim, and for such a purpose the precious promises covering life and service were given. Isaac Watts suggested:

> *So let our lips and lives express*
> *The holy Gospel we profess;*
> *So let our works and virtues shine,*
> *To prove the doctrine all Divine.*

Beside a Human Door

"I am the door." John 10:9.

Wordsworth had Lucy Gray in mind when he wrote:

—The sweetest thing that ever grew
Beside a human door.

When Jesus said, *"I am the door,"* he declared himself a "human door" through which all people could enter. What an understandable presentation of our adorable Redeemer this is! He is the ever-open door so that we can go in and out.

An ordinary door has two functions: it admits, yet excludes. We can open the door of our home and allow all welcome friends to enter. The same door, however, can be kept closed against others who have no wish to entertain. The allegory as used by Jesus of himself is consoling. He is the only entrance into the fold in which his sheep find safety, sustenance, and liberty. He is the only door into salvation now and heaven hereafter.

But the time is coming when, as the foolish virgins proved, the door will be closed. In this age of grace he is the ever-open door. His sorrow is that the door of the heart is fast closed against him, and his repeated knocking goes unheeded (Rev. 3:20). How unkind it is to keep him standing outside in the cold! To quote the Scottish Metrical Psalm 24:

Ye gates, lift up your heads on high;
ye doors that last for aye.
Be lifted up, that so the King
of glory enter may.

How assuring is his word, "If any man open the door, I will come in"! The blessed fact is that when he comes in he closes the door behind him.

The Want of a Nail

"I will fasten him as a nail in a sure place." *Isaiah 22:23.*

When Jesus became the recognized Son of a carpenter, then a carpenter himself, he learned all about the value and purpose of nails. Nails were daily *in* his hands, and when he came to die, cruel men drove nails *through* his hands. Among the varied and significant titles and types of Jesus, none is more expressive than that of a nail, for as such, he had been fastened by the Father in a sure or safe place. Does this not imply that he will never come loose, causing what depends upon him to fall? Applied to Jesus, the figure of a nail suggests fixity, the sense of security in his relationship to the throne of God.

We find nails useful in two ways, namely, for hanging things on and for binding things together. Isaiah says, "They shall hang on him all the glory of the Father's throne" (Isa. 22:24). Have you discovered Jesus as the nail on whom you can hang all that concerns you, which is but another way of casting all your care upon him? No weight is too heavy for him to carry. As nails join things together, so Jesus is the only nail able to unify his people and hold them together.

But Isaiah issued this warning: "The nail that is fastened in a sure place shall be removed." When this age of grace ends, a sinning world will no longer hear the joyful news that Jesus saves. Presently, he is its nail of salvation in the holy place (Ezra 9:8). Our hope is that when he does appear we shall see the print of the nails in his wonderful hands and also, as Shakespeare reminded us, in *1 Henry IV*:

> . . . *those blessed feet*
> *which fourteen hundred years ago were nail'd*
> *For our advantage on the bitter cross.*

The Throned Monarch Better Than His Crown

"In that day the Lord of Hosts will become a beautiful crown and a glorious diadem." *Isaiah 28:5*, ASB.

What a fascinating two-sided cameo of the Lord this is—a crown of glory and a diadem of beauty. On the one side we have the excellence, worth, sovereignty, and glory of the Lord. How visible this crown will be when he returns as the Lord of glory (Ps. 24)! On the other side we witness in the diadem of beauty the incomparable loveliness, luster, and radiance of our Lord: Who is like unto him, so glorious in holiness? Well might we pray with Charles Wesley, "Fill me, Radiancy divine!"

Too few of us have learned that he wishes us to have dominion with a "quality of mercy . . . [that] blesseth him that gives, and him that takes [and] becomes the throned monarch better than his crown" (Shakespeare, *The Merchant of Venice*)—achieving worth, radiance, and attractiveness of character. We sometimes sing, "Let the beauty of Jesus be seen in me," but is he, as the diadem of beauty, diademing our lives with his love and loveliness?

How ugly and despicable are the sins of the flesh when brought alongside him! Would that ours could be the ever-deep longing and determination to become his crown of glory and diadem of beauty! Such a combination of qualities delighting the sight and mind, however, cannot be acquired by human effort. They must be accepted from him who is altogether lovely and the source of all that is beautiful. An unknown writer gave us these lines:

> As some rare perfume in a vase of clay
> Pervades it with a fragrance not its own,
> So when Thou dwellest in a mortal soul,
> All Heaven's own sweetness seems around it thrown.

The Church's One Foundation

"For a foundation a stone, a tried stone, a precious corner stone, a sure foundation." *Isaiah 28:16.*

How different is the prophet's stable foundation to "the refuge of lies" which the ungodly fashion for their safety! Paul agreed with Isaiah when he called the Lord *a foundation*, for did he not say, "Other foundation can no man lay than that is laid, which is Jesus Christ" (I Cor. 3:11)? Thus the foundation of our faith is not a precept, but a Person, not a fact, but a figure, even him, who cannot be moved. This wonderful truth inspired Samuel J. Stone to pen his great hymn:

> *The Church's one foundation*
> *Is Jesus Christ her Lord;*
> *She is His new creation,*
> *By Spirit and the Word.*

The metaphor of foundation suggests the thought of stability or a solid base. Jesus, in his parable of the building of two houses, illustrated how the foundation made all the difference between them. One house was doubtless built all right, but the foundation was all wrong. Being of *sand*, it was not *sure* and fell when a storm arose. But the other house stood the test of the hurricane since it was built on rock. Jesus himself is our foundation on a tried stone, and John Newton wrote:

> *On the Rock of Ages founded,*
> *What can shake thy sure repose?*

Philosophies, precepts, morals, and axioms may be commendable in a way, but they do not offer a safe foundation on which a sinner may build. Life can only be secure and stable if built upon Jesus, the unmovable rock in a weary land. If rejected, he becomes "a rock of offense."

Sermons in Stones

"The stone which the builders rejected." I Peter 2:7.

Peter, quoting from Isaiah, wrote of Jesus as "a chief cornerstone, elect, precious," "the stone the builders rejected," "a stone of stumbling" to them which "stumble at the word" (I Pet. 2:6–8). How full of spiritual import this symbol of Jesus is! As the *chief cornerstone* he possesses peculiar honor in the most wonderful temple ever built.

As the *living stone* he is not an inert mass of particles as stones out of the ground, but a living and life-imparting stone. As the *elect stone* he came out of the council chamber of heaven as God's chosen one to die as the Savior for the salvation of a world of stony hearts. As the *precious stone* he is a jewel beyond compare. To all who receive and love him he is precious or, as the Scofield Reference Bible margin states, "He is the preciousness" since he sacrificed his precious blood to redeem us.

As a *stone of stumbling* he is the one over whom many will fall into the abyss of eternal despair since they disobeyed his word and warning. As the *stone or rock of offense* he is related to his ancient people, the Jews, the rulers of whom were ever offended because of his life and teaching. As the *stone cut out of the mountain* he warns of his judicial authority and power in crushing godless nations to powder. It is to be hoped that you are not among the builders trying to fashion a successful life by rejecting Jesus as your fountain stone. But if your hope is built on nothing less than Jesus' blood and righteousness, then when you finally see him, he will reward you with a *white stone.*

78

GAIETY
and
GLORY

And what is so rare as a day in June
Then, if ever, come perfect days;
Then Heaven tries earth if it be in tune,
And over it softly her warm ear lays.

—James Russell Lowell,
"Vision of Sir Launfal"

Build, Broad on the Roots of Things

"The Root of David." Revelation 5:5.

Robert Browning advised us to "burrow awhile and build, broad on the roots of things." John told us that Jesus, the root of divine things, is the only one to build broad upon. Is he, as the root of any matter, firmly embedded in the soil of your heart? In his prophetic portrayal of the messianic mission of Jesus, Isaiah described him as coming like "a root out of a dry ground," destitute of any comeliness, and when seen, undesired because of his lack of beauty (Isa. 53:2).

When Jesus entered his public messiahship, Jewish leaders could not see in him the kind of Messiah they expected. To them he was only a dead, dry root. His human life was obscure and humble, and those who rejected him as their Messiah could not find in him any resemblance to a stately tree, only one who was like a tender plant or a root struggling to exist in arid soil. We are to understand Jesus as the Root of David. Scripture often traces the human lineage of Jesus back to King David, whose root he was in relation to the throne and kingdom rights promised to David.

What possibilities are imprisoned in a root! Planted in suitable soil, it springs up into beauty or benefit for mankind. Jesus came as a root, and what fruit he has produced! In his parable of the sower he described how some seeds were scorched by the sun "because they had no root." Is Jesus deep in your heart as the Root? If so, then no sun can scorch you, and barrenness is impossible. Blessed be his name! None can dig him up, but sin can prevent him as the Root producing the fruit of the Spirit in our lives. He ever remains the root whence mercy ever flows.

Sanctuary within the Holier Blue

"Yet will I be to them a little sanctuary." *Ezekiel 11:16.*

In "The Ring and the Book" Robert Browning wrote these expressive lines:

> *Boldest of hearts that ever braved the sun,*
> *Took sanctuary within the holier blue,*
> *And sang a kindred soul out to his face,*
> *Yet human at the red-ripe of the heart.*

Is it not consoling to know that the Lord himself is our sanctuary within the holier blue of heaven! "He shall be for a sanctuary" (Isa. 8:14). Ezekiel assured those he wrote for that no matter in what country they found themselves they would find the Lord as a small sanctuary to whom they could gather.

Amid the turmoil of the street, busy cares of home, exacting responsibilities of business, or necessary travel, we have a sanctuary closer than breathing, nearer than hearts or feet. No sanctuary has ever surpassed the Temple Solomon built. For magnificence and marvel it was incomparable; yet where is it today? But our sanctuary never decays.

It is fitting and scriptural to gather in a house of worship, whether it be a simple or a cathedrallike structure. The sphere of worship, however, as Jesus taught the woman at the well, makes little difference. Many dear shut-in ones cannot journey to a sanctuary of stone; yet hidden from earth's eyes and from all earth's din and confusion, they take advantage of him who offers himself as a sanctuary. Are we not privileged to have a person as well as a place to draw nigh to? Although he calls himself "a *little* sanctuary," in him there is room enough for all who worship in spirit and in truth.

The Tide of Times

"At that time Jesus answered and said, I thank thee
O Father." *Matthew 11:25.*

The Gospel is replete with illustrations of the timeliness of Jesus who
was never before his time or after it. He knew the exact moment to
speak or act. To borrow Shakespeare's phrase in *Julius Caesar*, Jesus
studied "the tide of times." *At that time!* Matthew never forgot the
precise time Jesus uttered his prayer to the Father. The very hour never
vanished from his memory. Jesus had been speaking of his rejection,
and darkness around him was deepening into tragedy, but at that very
time he rose to exultant thanksgiving to God.

From then on the disciples began to watch the times of Jesus as if in
those very times there was a message for their hearts. For us, as well as
for the disciples, there is much spiritual profit in studying the timeliness
of Jesus. At the marriage feast of Cana he said to his mother, "Mine
hour is not yet come." Jesus meant that she must not interfere; when
the hour struck, he would perform his task.

This reiterated insistence on his *hour*, when others sought to hasten
or retard him, illustrates his perfect timeliness. He silenced people by
speaking of his hour. Jesus refused to let himself be hurried or, when
the hour struck, to be delayed. As he faced Calvary, he said, "Mine
hour is come." There was one perfect moment and one only. As one
reads the Gospel narrative, one cannot fail to be impressed with the
exquisite timeliness the words and works of Jesus were. His words were
timely, and yet they have proved timeless. Although they were occa-
sional, they are yet immortal. This is why at the very time of some
crisis or sorrow his words to our hearts are so timely, even though
centuries have passed since they were first uttered for the comfort of
others.

Songs of Deliverance

"There shall come out of Sion the Deliverer."
Romans 11:26.

It is amazing to discover that the term *deliver* and its cognates occur over seven hundred times in the Bible. In the majority of references divine deliverance is implicated, proving Scripture to be the Magna Carta of emancipation. Jesus was appointed and anointed to deliver the sin-bound. Authority over all flesh was given to him, as was every attribute of deity which he exercised for the deliverance of his own whenever they had need of his aid.

Happily we are not left to struggle against the pull of the old nature within; nor are we left to the mercy of humankind to deliver us. We look to Jesus who came to deliver us from all evil. To him we repair in every trial, assured that he will preserve us from any danger since it is his office to hear us, set us free, and bless us. As our Deliverer he performs in temporals as well as in spirituals, from internal and external foes.

More than ever in a Devil-driven world we need to cling to his title as the *Deliverer*, making use of him as such in preference to any other. We should apply to him *first* in every difficulty, rely on him with confidence in every need, and believe that he will deliver until his aid is no longer required. The promise is, "He shall deliver the in six troubles: yea, in seven there shall no evil touch thee" (Job 5:19). From an unidentified source we have the words:

> *Lord, Thou canst help when earthly armour faileth,*
> *Lord, Thou canst save when deadly sin assaileth,*
> *Lord, o'er Thy Rock nor death nor hell prevaileth,*
> *Grant us Thy peace, Lord.*

Power Which Seems Omnipotent

"Upholding all things by the word of his power."
Hebrews 1:3.

Shelley wrote of those who "defy Power which seems omnipotent," but the power of God *is* omnipotent. Christ's omnipotence extends to every realm, for all power is his in heaven and on earth. He unfolds not some things but *all* things by his authoritative Word. Where the word of such a king is, there is power, and one sovereign Lord holds the reins of creation, redemption, history, prophecy, and personal life in his almighty hand.

Sometimes we hear it said, "Why, the world is going to pieces!" Broken it may be by wickedness and war, vice and violence, but it is still among the *"all"* things upheld by his power, for he never ceases to do according to his will among the inhabitants of earth. He overrules as well as rules and is therefore still able to change wrath to praise of him.

In the narrower world of our own lives do we believe in his power to uphold the daily things concerning us? Do we believe that, as of old, he can still speak and it is done? Does not trouble assail us when we take the control out of his hands and transfer it to our own hands? Did he not warn his own, "Without me ye can do nothing"? What folly it is to try to do and be something apart from him! Paul was very careful to say that it was only through Christ and his omnipotent strength that he could do all things. Job affirmed that the Lord is "excellent in power" and can do "everything" (Job 37:23, 42:2). Problems, difficulties, and needs may face you today and seem almost insurmountable. Do not panic or despair. By faith, rest in his power to prevail on your behalf, and you will prove that he is able to accomplish far more than you could ask or think.

Crowding in Their Heavy Burdens at the Narrow Gate

"Bear ye one another's burdens, and so fulfil the law of Christ." *Galatians 6:2.*

There is a sense in which all saints are among the *porters* that Shakespeare depicted in *Henry V* as unloading their heavy burdens at the gate. Paul urged us to make the burdens of others our own, irrespective of the personal load we carry, if we would be like Jesus whose law or custom it was to shoulder the weighty loads of others. Are we not told that he *bore* the sin of the world? He carried our sorrows and shouldered our infirmities. That heavy cross he was made to carry as he trudged to Calvary was our burden, for he was going out to die as our substitute.

Experimentally, do we know what it is to cast our burden upon this burden-bearing Lord? Said the psalmist, "Cast thy burden upon the Lord, and he shall sustain thee" (Ps. 55:22). The Scofield Reference Bible margin gives *gift* for "burden," or as the New American Standard Bible has it, "What He has given you." Who thinks of a burden as a *gift*? Is it not rather something to be rid of as quickly as possible? Yet any burden is a gift from the Lord if it results in drawing us nearer to himself and opens our eyes to the truth that he not only bears the burden but its bearer.

Whatever burden he may permit is *light*. But the question is, Are we emulating the Master in the art of burden-bearing? Is it our joy to lift the load of others? True, there are some burdens we cannot share; yet there are others we can help to carry. We live twice over when, Christlike, we make it easier for some heavy-laden heart to walk with a lighter step. We may heed the advice of a Sankey hymn:

> *Hearts growing a-weary with heavier woe*
> *Now droop amid the darkness—go, comfort them, go!*
> *Go bury thy sorrow, let others be blest;*
> *Go give them the sunshine, tell Jesus the rest.*

The Dear Remembrance of His Dying Lord

"Remember Jesus Christ." "In remembrance of me."
2 Timothy 2:8; 1 Corinthians 11:24.

Edmund Spenser, quaint poet of the sixteenth century, wrote of a saint:

> *But on his breast a bloody cross he bore,*
> *The dear remembrance of his dying Lord.*

Knowing how faulty the human memory is and how soon we are likely to forget, Jesus left us blessed tokens of remembrance of his agony in the broken bread and outpoured wine. J. R. Miller told of a mother who lost her longed-for baby and would constantly go to a drawer and take out the baby's shoes and clothes, fondly remembering the little one taken from her.

Jesus constituted the Supper to keep us in unfailing remembrance of his dying love. This is why the Holy Feast means very much to those who love him. As Alexander Smellie expressed it, "In the weekdays with their work and worry, a hundred interlopers hide my dying and undying Friend from me. But when the fair white cloth is spread, I see once more the Lord Who is all my Boast: Him I see, and none beside."

If remembrance is a paradise from which we need not be driven, then our constant remembrance of Jesus himself and of all he has accomplished on our behalf will bring us a daily paradise. His declaration is that he never forgets: "Yet will I not forget thee." How can he fail to remember us when our very names are written upon the palms of his hands? May we never be guilty of forgetting him who has us in everlasting remembrance. Thus we can sing with an unknown writer:

> *Our Master's love remember,*
> *Exceeding great and free;*
> *Lift up thy heart in gladness,*
> *For He remembers thee.*

The Sweetest of All Singers

"When they had sung an hymn." *Mark 14:26.*

How moving is Longfellow's "Hiawatha's Lamentation":

> *He is dead, the sweet musician!*
> *He is the sweetest of all singers!*
> *He has gone from us for ever,*
> *He has moved a little nearer*
> *To the Master of all music,*
> *To the Master of all singing!*
> *O my brother, Chibiabos!*

Without doubt Jesus is the master of all music and of all singing. Was he not one of that singing company of which Mark reminded us? Jesus had just broken bread with his disciples. Having explained the mystic significance of the bread and wine, he turned aside from the chamber and stepped out with his own into the dark night.

Where were their footsteps taking them? "They went to the Mount of Olives." Their faces were set toward the garden and Golgotha, but the marvel is that they faced the sorrowful future with a song. Surely it is not irreverent to suggest that Jesus, "the Master of all singing," led the chorus on that dark night. Possibly some of the Degree Psalms (120–134) he knew so well formed the hymn he prompted the small company to sing. We know he died that he might give us songs in the night, as he gave Paul and Silas when at the midnight hour, suffering in a filthy cell, they "sang praises unto God." Pain could not silence their song. Gladness banished their grief.

Francis Beaumont and John Fletcher, joint poets of the early seventeenth century, wrote:

> *Come sing now, sing; for I know ye sing well,*
> *I see ye have a singing face.*

Whether or not we have a singing face, let us be sure that we have a singing heart.

The Second Chariot

"Pharoah made Joseph to ride in the second chariot."
Genesis 41:43.

Although laden with spiritual import, this detail in the fascinating biography of Joseph, Jacob's favorite son, is generally overlooked. First, it displays Joseph's rise from prison to palace and to a position of second importance in Egypt. Many have gone from a palace to a prison, but very few from prison to palace; yet Joseph went through the experience gracefully.

Many evidences of royalty became his. The *ring* was a token of friendship between Pharoah and Joseph; the *chain of office*, a symbol of authority; the *white robe*, an official recognition of his purity; marriage to a *prince's daughter* and the chariot enabling him to travel through Egyptian provinces, tokens of the authority of a royal personage. No fleshy ambition brought Joseph to his high office. It came as the reward of nobility of character. This godly ruler had no aspiration for the *first* chariot but was content with the *second*. Upright and innocent, he had suffered far too long to gender ambition for national prestige. Although he rode in the second chariot as the savior of Egypt, he exercised more power and influence than the Pharoah riding in the first chariot. Joseph's trust was not in chariots because he could always hear, as Andrew Marvell of the seventeenth century wrote in "To His Coy Mistress":

> *Time's wingéd chariot hurrying near,*
> *And yonder all before us lie*
> *Deserts of vast eternity.*

Are you content with riding in the *second* chariot or occupying the *second* place, believing that character is greater than any chariot and that only those who humble themselves are exalted? It is often so hard for us to learn that the only way *up* is *down*, that only those who abase themselves earn the right to exaltation.

Homeless near a Thousand Homes

"The Son of man hath not where to lay his head."
Matthew 8:20.

How truly descriptive of Jesus are the lines of Wordsworth in "Guilt and Sorrow":

> *And homeless near a thousand homes I stood,*
> *And near a thousand tables pined and wanted food.*

I am moved by Samuel Crossman's remarks on the humiliation and poverty of Jesus in a verse of his hymn "My Song Is Love Unknown":

> *In life, no house, no home*
> *My Lord on earth might have;*
> *In death, no friendly tomb*
> *But what a stranger gave.*
> *What may I say?*
> *Heav'n was his home:*
> *But mine the tomb*
> *Wherein He lay.*

Jesus spoke of the way inferior creatures were well-provided for. *Foxes* have their holes, and *birds* of the air, taking no care of themselves yet taken care of, have their nests. Their Creator, however, did not know the convenience of a certain resting place he could call *home*, or place of repose. Such a settlement was not his, not even a pillow of his own upon which to lay his head.

Christ here calls Himself *the Son of Man*, a Son of Adam, partaker of flesh and blood. Matthew Henry said, "He glories in His condescension towards us, to testify His love towards us, and to teach us a holy contempt of the world, and a continual regard to another world. Christ was thus poor to sanctify and sweeten poverty to His people." Paul knew what it was to share the homelessness of his Master, for he wrote of having no "certain dwelling-place." The main thing is to know that we have given Jesus a home in our hearts.

He Shareth in Our Gladness

"Jesus rejoiced in the Holy Spirit." *Luke 10:21,* RV.

Cecil F. Alexander, unique composer of children's hymns, in his appealing verses, "Once in Royal David's City," described the tears and smiles of Jesus when he was "little, weak, and helpless" and then said:

> And He feeleth for our sadness,
> And He shareth in our gladness.

The Gospels may not record his laughing with joy; yet his gladsomeness is only too evident. The word Luke used for *rejoiced* is very strong and expresses exaltation and ecstatic delight. What caused this deep thrill of joy to the Savior's heart? Did he not praise the Father for the *method* which he had chosen for the proclamation and establishment of his kingdom? More generally, despite all the sorrows that lay upon his heart, and the heaviness of the Cross he had to bear, there can be little doubt that Jesus impressed people as a very gladsome person.

When he spoke about his joy, nobody had to ask him what he meant, for he was the embodiment of it. He called himself the *bridegroom,* and who ever saw a bridegroom with a long face? What, then, was the secret of the gladness of this Man of Sorrows? How did he maintain, even in the darkest hours, the joyful, undisturbed, radiant heart?

He was supremely faithful in his appointed vocation, never swerving from the fulfillment of God's will. He shone in the tranquil radiance of fidelity. One of the deepest attributes of duty is that the doing of it always leads to gladness. Only thus can we be glad in the Lord. Carlyle said, "Give me the man who sings at his work." Do we have a gladsome mind?

Christ Is Thy Strength

"Gathered together in my Name." *Matthew 18:20.*

Whenever and wherever the saints gather for worship, such is only acceptable when they meet for fellowship in his name. Alas, multitudes assemble for worship on Sunday, not in his name, but in their own denominational name. "Christ is thy strength," wrote John S. B. Monsell in "Fight of Faith." If Jesus is not recognized as Savior and as a King whose name has strength, or if all that belongs to him is denied, such as his virgin birth, his deity, his miracles, his efficacious death and resurrection, even though the apparent worshipers have a form of religion, how can they be said to have gathered in his name?

Matthew Henry's wise comment should be considered by every church member: "When we come together, to worship God in a dependence upon the Spirit and grace of Christ . . . having an actual regard to Him as our Way to the Father, and our Advocate with the Father, then we are met together in His Name . . . [and] are encouraged with an assurance of the presence of Christ, *There am I in the midst of them.*" How seriously we have departed from God's New Testament principles honoring worship! Jennie Garnett wrote:

> *Here in Thy Name we are gather'd,*
> *Come and revive us, O Lord:*
> *"There shall be showers of blessing,"*
> *Thou hast declared in Thy Word.*

As those who bear his name, let us ever honor it by lips and life, doing nothing that would detract from its worth and power.

The Continual Dew of Thy Blessing

"The Lord be with you all." *2 Thessalonians 3:16.*

How unique Paul is in his pronouncement of salutations and benedictions! The apostle loved to greet the saints and then dismiss them with a blessing such as the one before us which portrays Jesus as the ever-present companion of his people. Cervantes, of the sixteenth century, gave us the proverb, "Where there's no more bread, boon companions melt away." This may be true as far as some earthly companions are concerned, but in Jesus we have a companion who never leaves us and who, when there is no more bread, is able to provide it. Repeatedly, we are reminded of his abiding presence. He is always at hand, consoling our hearts with his blessing and bounty. We need nothing more to make us safe and serene, and we could wish nothing better for ourselves and our friends than the promise of his unfailing companionship.

It is the presence of God that makes heaven to be heaven, and this will make this earth to be like heaven. But note who it is that accompanies us. It is the Lord. Paul's benediction then implies that as the Lord he is the master of every situation. His miracles prove that he is able to undertake for us accordingly. Further, his lordship is not exercised on behalf of a few elect souls but for *all* who are his, even for you and me, simple, ordinary, and inconspicuous though we may be. All he is and has can be appropriated by each and all.

May we be spared negligence in taking advantage of the abundant provision of such an ever-present companion on life's pilgrimage. As daily we face "the trivial round, the common task," is ours the privilege and joy of knowing what it is to have Jesus walking with and talking to us? Do others detect the fragrance of our unseen Master?

An Incomparable Storyteller

"Without a parable spake he not unto them."
Matthew 13:34.

In *Tales of a Traveler* Washington Irving wrote, "I am always at a loss to know how much to believe of my own stories." Jesus had every faith in the stories he told, for all of them were a picturesque way of declaring the truth people needed to hear. And what a matchless storyteller Jesus was! No wonder the common people gladly listened to his preaching. For naturalness, conciseness, color, and effect his parables, metaphors, and illustrations are without equal. If a parable is an earthly story with a heavenly meaning, then he knew how to draw from a wide range of subjects, stories, or parables so full of spiritual import.

The story of the husbandman smote the consciences of those Pharisees who listened to it with deep interest. They knew that Jesus told the story against them, and had it not been for his popularity among the people, they would have taken him prisoner.

All who are called to preach and teach the Word can learn precious lessons on the art of illustration from the oral ministry of Jesus. Usually his illustrations were taken from human life and were never used simply for the sake of telling them. Alas, some preachers are guilty of padding their sermons with too many stories, containing no connection with their main thought. Illustrations should always function as windows letting the light in on truth being expressed. The function of a good illustration is to make clear, and it is this that makes Jesus the storyteller *par excellence.*

To the Tent-royal of Their Emperor

"Prince of the kings of the earth." Revelation 1:5.

An emperor is a supreme monarch or the ruler of an empire in which lesser kings may be yielding him obedience. Among the many titles Christ possesses, none is so expressive as prince, monarch, or controller of all earthly kings. We have Shakespeare'e saying in *2 Henry IV*, that "Uneasy lies the head that wears a crown." But on Christ's head are many crowns speaking of universal sovereignty; yet his head is never uneasy. He never has any fear that he will lose his multiple crown to a usurper. As the King of kings he will yet reign as world emperor with no dread of a rival, and his kingdom will last until moons shall wax and wane no more.

Earthly kings are sometimes deposed, shorn of their power, or assassinated. In Victorian times Britain was an empire, holding sway over vast dominions with their rulers, but no longer. Christ's empire will never shrink, for "of his government there shall be no end" (Isa. 9:6). His reign is to be universal, prosperous, and perpetual, with multitudes crying, "Hail to Thee, Thou princely King!" From a hymn by James Watts we shall sing:

> *To Him shall endless prayer be made,*
> *And princes throng to crown His head,*
> *His name like sweet perfume shall rise*
> *With every morning sacrifice.*

While our hearts thrill at the thought of the universal coronation he is to receive, the present question of paramount importance is, Have you crowned him king of your life? If he is not Lord of all within your life, he is not Lord at all. Does he reign supreme, without a rival, in your heart? If not, then give him his coronation as king of your life.

I Conquer but to Save

"Our Saviour Jesus Christ who hath abolished death."
2 Timothy 1:10.

What a glorious gospel is proclaimed in this verse as a whole! Here Jesus emerges as a conqueror with garments bloodstained after treading the winepress alone to save a lost world. Existing before the world began, he appeared among men in order to redeem them from sin and bless them with his eternity. Calvary was a grim conflict, but as the Lord of life he abolished death. By dying, death he slew. Through his grief and gospel brought life and immortality to light.

Until Jesus' death and resurrection there was no full revelation of the afterlife. True, "life and immortality" were hidden in Old Testament Scriptures, but Jesus banished their obscurity and made them shine. As the result of the cross and the empty tomb, the shadows have fled away, and we now have clear guidance as to where we are bound.

He abolished death! This is a marvelous truth, but saints and sinners still die, and countless graves gain the victory. How then did Jesus abolish death? First, he proved himself to be its conqueror when he rose from the grave. Second, he abolished death by robbing it of its sting and of its climax in "the second death"—the terrible condition of all who die in their sin! May we be found basking in the full light the Gospel sheds on all that awaits us when our bodies return to their native element. Said Jesus, "He that believeth in me shall never die." D. W. Whittle wrote a hymn with which we may identify:

> *Dying with Jesus, by death reckoned mine;*
> *Living with Jesus, a new life divine;*
> *Looking to Jesus till glory doth shine*
> *Moment by moment, O Lord, I am Thine.*

A Privileged Association

"Why persecutest thou me . . . I am Jesus whom thou persecutest." *Acts 9:4–5.*

This historic, memorable chapter opens with Saul breathing out threatenings and slaughter against the disciples of Jesus; yet when smitten with a heavenly, blinding light, this hater of "the way" heard a voice from heaven calling his name and asking, "Why persecutest me?" When Saul requested the speaker to identify himself, he received the reply, "I am Jesus whom thou persecutest."

Is there not a precious truth in such a revelation? Ignorant Saul thought he was persecuting a small band of poor, deluded religious zealots, little thinking it was one in heaven that he was all the while insulting. "Why persecutest thou *me*?" Jesus was not on earth among those saints to be brought in chains to Jerusalem, but because he and his own are one, Saul, in persecuting the disciples, was persecuting their Lord himself. Graciously, he identifies himself with his suffering disciples and takes what is done against them as done against himself. In effect, Jesus said, "Persecute them, any of the members of my body, and I, as the head, likewise endure the same affliction. Touch them, and you touch the apple of my eye."

The same precious truth of this privileged identification or association is emphasized when Jesus said, "Inasmuch as ye have done it unto one of the least of these . . . ye have done it unto me" (Matt. 25:40). When we suffer for his cause and sake, may consolation be ours that Jesus suffers with us. Because he has all power in heaven and on earth, he can deal effectively with those who persecute us since he is still able to transform blasphemers into believers. The union making Christ and the redeemed as one is the constant theme of the Gospels and the Epistles. Hymn writer James George Deck asked:

> Lord Jesus, are we one with Thee?
> Oh height! Oh depth of love!
> With Thee we died upon the tree,
> In Thee we live above.

The Eternal Beam

"Now unto the King eternal." *1 Timothy 1:17.*

The description John Milton gave of Lucifer in *Paradise Lost* is truer of our Blessed Lord:

> *. . . Th' Eternal co-eternal beam,*
> *May I express Thee unblamed? Since God is light,*
> *But never but is unapproach light*
> *Dwelt from Eternity*

While Paul's great and glorious portrait presents our heavenly sovereign in a fivefold way, it is as the "King Eternal" or of the Ages that we are to consider. To apply Shakespeare's lines in *Macbeth* to Jesus, he is:

> *. . . Mine eternal jewel*
> *Given to the common enemy of man.*

We know that Jesus was born a King and will yet be seen as the King of kings, but how is he the *eternal king*? The answer is simple: Jesus was a King *before* his birth and therefore a King *at* his birth. Did he not come as "the Father of eternity" (Isa. 9:6, 7)? Jesus lived before he was born. Majesty, honor, and glory were his in the past eternity. Thus before God gave him to die for the salvation of his common enemies, he could say of his "eternal jewel," "Yet have I set my King upon my holy hill of Zion" (Ps. 2:6). As the blessed and only Potentate his was no acquired or anticipated sovereignty. It goes back before the beginning of time when Jesus dwelt in eternity. Did he not affirm, "Before Abraham was, I am" (John 8:58)?

From everlasting he was established as the daily delight of his Father, rejoicing always before him (Prov. 8:22–31). John went beyond the beginning of creation when he wrote, "In the beginning was the Word, and the Word was with God, and the Word was God" (John 1:1). Jesus came as the eternal Word.

There Grows the Flower of Peace

"The Lord of peace." *2 Thessalonians 3:16.*

Henry Vaughan, religious poet of the seventeenth century, in his verses on peace spoke of one born in a manger as "Sweet Peace is crown'd with smiles." He went on to describe him as "the One, Who never changes, thy life, thy care" and then said:

> *If thou canst get but thither,*
> *There grows the flower of peace,*
> *The rose that cannot wither,*
> *Thy fortress and thy ease.*

In the apostolic benediction of peace several aspects appear. First, Paul named Jesus as the *Lord of peace.* He is the source of all true peace; he is our peace in a person. Second, he is the *giver of peace,* personal and universal. As "the Prince of Peace" he is princely in his bestowal on those willing to receive his gift. Third, this peace can be ours *always.* Whether our experiences are tranquil or turbulent makes no difference, for his blood ever whispers peace within. Did he not say that we may meet with tribulation in the world but that there is ever peace in him for those who are *in* him? Fourth, Paul, in his benediction, reminded us that the Lord's peace can be ours "always *by all means.*"

Peace comes to us directly from its prince through his Word and by his Spirit. Sometimes the most unusual experiences contribute to our peace of heart. Samson is not the only one to discover honey in the carcass of a lion! Is yours an inner peace nothing can disturb or destroy? If we would constantly experience his perfect peace in this dark world of sin, our mind must be stayed upon him in whom we profess to trust. Only as we are stayed upon Jehovah do we find tranquillity and rest.

The Shadow of a Great Rock

"The spiritual Rock that followed them . . . was Christ."
1 Corinthians 10:4.

We usually think of a rock as an immovable object, like the Rock of Gibraltar. Many famous rocks have remained steadfast through millenniums, never moving an inch. But Paul reminded us of a rock on the march, for as the Israelites journeyed through the wilderness, the rock of refreshment followed them. Such a rock was not something but *someone.* "That Rock was Christ." Charles John Ellicott commented, "As Christ was 'God manifest in the flesh,' in the New Dispensation, so God manifested in the Rock—the Source of sustaining life—was the Christ of the Old Dispensation. The Jews had become familiar with the thought of God as a rock, 1 Sam. 2:2 etc. The point the Apostle brings forward is that of the abiding presence of God."

As pilgrims, is it not comforting that thirst will never afflict us in the desert? No matter where we may go, the life-giving rock follows. The margin has it, "The Rock went with them." Thus anywhere and at all times we can stoop down and drink and live. How mobile Jesus is! He ever moves with his own who are built on him as the rock, and the water he gives is sufficient for their need. May we be found constantly appropriating him as the rock whose shelter and sustenance are unfailing. Emily Brontë could write of those:

So surely anchored on
The stedfast rock of immortality.

Are you safely anchored in such a rock in this weary land? Can you sing out of a redeemed heart, along with William O. Cushing, "Thou blest 'Rock of Ages,' I'm hiding in Thee"? He only is our shade by day and our defense by night.

To Give Thanks Is Good, and to Forgive

"The same night in which he was betrayed."
1 Corinthians 11:23.

Extolling nature as being "full of blessings," Wordsworth gave us this expressive sentiment in "Tintern Abbey":

Knowing that Nature never did betray
The heart that loved her.

The tragedy of our Lord's last hours was the way in which one of the disciples he loved betrayed him. While a good deal of mystery shrouds the choice of Judas and his dastardly act of selling his Master for thirty pieces of silver, the truth we should never lose sight of is that Jesus himself carried no animosity in his heart toward his betrayer. What particularly interests us in the phrase *"the same night* in which he was betrayed" is what happened shortly after Jesus was sold with a kiss. "The same night . . . he gave thanks." Think of it! Gratitude followed the committal of Judas' foul crime! Immediate thanks dried up any thought of anger, bitterness, or revenge. This was the same Jesus who taught his own to agree with their adversary *while in the way.*

Wrong feelings are like babies: the longer we nurse them, the larger they grow. The longer we take to forgive those who injure us, the harder it becomes to forgive. Have you been wronged by someone who is close to you, as Judas was to Jesus? Then remember the same-night attitude of your Master and give thanks even for a bitter cup. "To give thanks is good, and to forgive," wrote Swinburne. The way in which we immediately respond to any form of betrayal by others is an indication of our likeness to him who is ever ready to forgive. We repeat with an unknown writer:

Knowest thou Him?—Who forgave,
  with the Crown of Thorns on His temples?
Earnestly prayed for His foes, for His murderers,—
  say dost thou know Him?
Ah! thou confessest His name,
  so follow likewise His example!

105

An Interpreter of the Cogitations Thereof

"Open the seals thereof; for thou wast slain."
Revelation 5:9.

The above title from Ecclesiasticus is certainly true of Jesus, the redeemer-interpreter. The worshipful host, singing the new song, extols the worthiness of the slain lamb to take the Book and open its seals or reveal its fascinating contents. Such ability and authority of Jesus to unveil the judgments and the joys contained in the last book of the Bible are based upon his redemptive work at Calvary, "For thou wast slain." As the central truth of the entire Bible is the cross, only he who died upon it can unfold its mystery and message. As the crucified, risen Lord he was able to expound in all the Scriptures the things concerning himself. Thus as the redeemer he alone has the right to function as the revealer.

If we would know how to take the Book and open its seals, then, as with the divine interpreter, there must come a death. Sin and self must be slain if we desire to discover the treasures of the Word. Are we worthy to take the Book and break its seals? Does our life correspond to its precepts? An ever-expanding knowledge of the secrets of the Lord depends upon obedience. If I disobey what I discover today, the Spirit will not grant me further and fuller light tomorrow. Disobedience closes the door of revelation; death, identification with the death of the cross, opens it. Is this not what Job meant when he prayed, "That which I see not, teach thou me: if I have done iniquity, I will do no more"? Revelation results in sanctification. The more we gaze upon divine holiness as set forth in Scripture, the deeper our sense of personal unworthiness. Yet, what the vision reveals of sin, the blood can cleanse.

All Combin'd in Beauty's Worthiness

"Worthy is the Lamb that was slain." *Revelation 5:12.*

I have no hesitation in taking Christopher Marlowe's phrase and applying it to Jesus who combined in all his virtues "beauty's worthiness." Although he was the one "of whom the world was not worthy," the vast angelic host, along with the living creatures and the elders of which John wrote, exalt his worthiness because he became the Lamb. This ascription of praise is fitting, for Jesus is worthy all he requires, all we can give, all his people have done for him or suffered in his cause. The Book of Revelation provides us with many striking cameos of Jesus as the *Lamb*. In the verse before us he is the "worthy Lamb."

Think of all he is worthy to receive as the Lamb, "freshly slain" as the original suggests! *Power* is his—all power in heaven and on earth. *Riches* are his whether spiritual or material. The wealth in every mine belongs to him. *Wisdom* is his, for he became wisdom personified, and his teachings contain the highest wisdom. *Strength* is his. Ultimately the strength of the strongest vanishes, as Samson experienced, but Jesus' strength remains undiminished because it is eternal. *Honor* is his. Every knee, Paul said, will yet acknowledge him as Lord. *Glory* is his. With his ascension came the restoration of the glory for which he prayed (John 17:1–4). Before long the whole earth will be filled with his glory. *Blessing* is his. The fullness of every blessing is now his to bestow. Because he became the Lamb, all he is and has can be ours. Sir Isaac Watts recognized:

> *Jesus is worthy to receive Honour and power divine;*
> *And blessings, more than we can give, Be, Lord, for ever Thine.*

It will take all eternity to magnify and praise his intrinsic worth.

A Coiner of Sweet Words

"The words of our Lord Jesus Christ." *1 Timothy 6:3.*

The magic power of words to blast or bless has been dealt with by many writers. Samuel Johnson would have us know that "words are the daughters of earth, and that things are the sons of Heaven." Alexander Pope wrote of one "grac'd as thou art with all the pow'r of words." Robert Louis Stevenson would have us remember that "bright is the ringing of words, when the right man rings them." Tennyson, who was a master of words, reckoned that "words, like Nature, half reveal—And half conceal the soul within." Thomas Gray wrote the line, "Thoughts that breathe, words that burn."

I take, however, the phrase Matthew Arnold used of another writer as "a coiner of sweet words" to describe the wonderful words of life that Jesus, a wizard of short, simple words, uttered. He was not afflicted with a barren superfluity of words and did not conform to those Philip Massinger described as being "All words / And no performance!"

As the prince of preachers Jesus knew how to seek out acceptable words which were as goads and as nails fastened in a sure place. His lips were like lilies, dropping sweet-smelling myrrh, and like a thread of scarlet uttering comely speech (Song of Sol. 4:3, 5:13, 16). How privileged were the multitudes to listen to the gracious words proceeding out of his mouth! Vain and idle words never left the lips into which grace had been poured. Every word was a benediction. He was never verbose or guilty of using unnecessary or long and involved words. Each word was rightly coined and timed and shot as an arrow to a given target.

Life for us would be saved much of its friction if only we would set a watch upon our lips. All our words will be acceptable to God if only we "weigh them in a balance, and make a door and a bar for our mouth" (Ecclus. 28:15). How apt are the lines of George MacDonald: "Thou Comforter! be with me as Thou wert When first I longed for words, to be A radiant garment for my thought, like Thee."

May of Thee Be Plenteously Rewarded

"The Lord, the righteous judge." 2 Timothy 4:8.

From the Book of Common Prayer we gather the petition that God's faithful people may be found "plenteously bringing forth the fruits of good works, and may of Thee be plenteously rewarded." Through all his arduous service for the Master, Paul kept before him the judgment seat and its rewards. The smile and benediction of the judge at the end of the day was the apostle's constant incentive. One look from this righteous adjudicator, and the sound of his voice saying, "Well done, good and faithful servant," spurred on the apostle, enabling him to be indifferent to his sufferings for Christ's sake. This was the prize of his high calling he strove to attain.

Paul knew that because the Lord is the *righteous* judge he would assist his labors and longings for what they were worth and reward him accordingly. Being the judge he is, the Lord cannot deny any servant of his any earned reward. Ours is the assurance that if we are faithful to him unto death the judge of all the earth will do right. If we have plenteously brought forth the fruits of good works, ours will be a plenteous reward. There is, of course, a great difference between gifts and rewards. A gift is bestowed, gratis. It would cease to be a gift if we had to work for it. But a reward has to be earned. Alas, many at the judgment seat will be saved because of their reception of the gift of God's salvation but will be rewardless because of a lost life.

Do we share Paul's confidence that an unfading crown is laid up for us? By God's grace and power are we pressing toward a full reward? May we be spared the sorrow of standing before the judge with a saved soul but a lost life. May ours be a full reward.

Without an Original There Can Be No Imitation

"Be ye imitators of God, as dear children."
Ephesians 5:1, RV.

The apostle Paul set before the Ephesians, and us, an astonishing yet reasonable demand, namely, to be godlike in all our ways, works, and words. As a child watches his or her father and unconsciously becomes like him in habits and nature, so God sets the standard for his redeemed children to follow. As he is and does, so are we to be and do. The word *followers* in the Authorized Version means "imitators." "Therefore be imitators of God as beloved children."

At the outset let it be said that by ourselves we cannot emulate the divine example. This is no mere human effort to strive in every possible way to be like God who proposes himself to us as our pattern. But he not only presents himself for our imitation. He imparts the grace and power whereby we can exhibit all of his divine virtues. Christ left us an example to follow his step, but he is within us enabling us to walk even as he walked. An unknown essayist of the eighteenth century said that "without an original there can be no imitation." Christ is our original and by his indwelling Spirit helps us to imitate him.

Horace, in his *Epistles*, wrote of those in Roman days, "O imitators, ye slavish herd." But as the imitators of God we are not driven by fear and force to imitate him. Certainly, he commands us to imitate him, but our relation to him requires it; and our peace is involved in it. From the context it would seem as if the one attribute above others, recommended for our imitation, is God's *love*. As his dear children we are to "walk in love." This should be the divine principle to practice. Alas, however, we are bad imitators of the original when we come to loving all that he loves. May grace be ours to exhibit more godlikeness in a godless world.

Escaped Even As a Bird out of the Snare

"God . . . will with the temptation make also the way of
escape." *1 Corinthians 10:13*, RV.

While God permits temptation, he does not provide it. He allows the
enemy to try us in order that we might be sifted. God suffered his well-
beloved Son to be tempted of the Devil, but he emerged from the grim
conflict with his sinlessness unimpaired. God's *way of escape* from
temptation then consists in preventing the attack of the enemy or in
divesting temptation of its force. Whether or not we are conscious of
it, God prepares you and me to bear the siege before which, if it were
not for his faithfulness, we would fall to the foe.

During the hour of temptation, God is at hand and, with the trial
under his control, adjusts it to our capacity. We can trust God for
victory over Satan because God makes the temptation flee through his
omnipotence. We emerge from the contest richer in humility since we
have discovered our own feebleness. We are also richer in faith, for the
struggle with our adversary draws us near the captain of our salvation.
We are richer too in sympathy because of our manifold temptations, for
experience enables us to guide and help fellow believers who are being
assailed by the enemy.

Without fail, God makes the way of escape for us, but we must seek
it by abounding in prayer, by guarding against any shameful surrender,
and above all by depending upon the indwelling Spirit who is able to
make us more than conquerors. Paul would have us remember that our
sheet anchor in seasons of testing is the faithfulness of God. The
apostle gave us one of those blessed *buts* of Scripture: "But God is
faithful who will not suffer you to be tempted above that ye are able"
(I Cor. 10:13). We are encouraged by an unknown author to:

> *Trust on! the danger presses, Temptation strong is near*
> *Over life's dangerous rapids, He shall thy passage steer.*

More Than Enough, for Nature's Ends

"God has dealt graciously with me, and because I have plenty." *Genesis 33:9, 11*, ASB.

Like the hired servants in our Lord's parable of the prodigal son, both Esau and Jacob had bread enough and to spare. The Authorized Version reads, "Jacob said, I have enough, or I have all things." I prefer, however, the translation given above from the American Standard Bible. David Mallet, a lesser known Scottish poet who died in 1765, left us this verse:

> *O grant me, Heaven, a middle state,*
> *Neither too humble nor too great;*
> *More than enough, for nature's ends,*
> *With something left to treat my friends.*

The contrast between Jacob leaving home and returning to it years later is most striking. He was forced to leave his father's house and took nothing with him but a staff. But the Lord greatly prospered him, as Esau could see in the large family and abundant possessions of his brother. Yet the kindness of Esau's approach after the long estrangement and the grace and goodness of God led Jacob to say, "I have plenty."

Spiritually, is our cup full and running over? As objects of Jehovah's everlasting love we are entitled to all the riches he offers. In him there is more than enough to make us holy, to fill us with gratitude, to fill angels with wonder, and to fill the Devil with envy. Why then do we live as spiritual paupers when there is bread enough and to spare in our Father's house? If God is an all-sufficient store, why not buy of him all we need without money and without price? Plenteous in mercy and grace, God invites us to partake of his bounty and live as those who are rich in faith. David could say, "My cup floweth over" (Ps. 23:5). Is yours the overflowing cup?

His Life Is a Watch

"I say unto all, Watch." *Mark 13:37.*

This clarion call of Jesus must be interpreted in light of the parable of the men taking a journey into a far country but who may return at any time. It apparently applies to our being watchful in view of the return of Jesus himself. Oliver Goldsmith depicted "the broken soldier" who was prompt at every call and who "watch'd and wept, he pray'd and felt for all."

Is this our attitude as we anticipate his glorious appearing? As we watch and wait, are we weeping over, and praying for, the multitudes of erring ones around us? John Keats wrote of the bright steadfast star hanging aloft, "Watching, with eternal lids apart." May this be the character of our watching for the dawning of "the Bright and Morning Star."

The coming of the Savior is the grand object of our hope and should be our daily desire and prayer. In wisdom and mercy God has purposely concealed the time of his Son's return. He commands us to be *awake* and, as watchmen, to keep awake as night approaches. By the Spirit's aid we should discern the signs of Christ's return and at the same time watch over our daily conduct, thus being ready to hail his arrival. We should watch and walk as we wish death or Jesus to find us. We should transact all our affairs as though the Master were at the door, as he may well be. Surely you would not like Jesus to come and find you idle, contentious, at enmity with a fellow believer, murmuring over God's providence, indulging in any sin. May your life, as Swinburne put it, be a watch. The Master calls you to watch and pray. Wrote an unknown author:

> Passing along the street—Among those thronging footsteps,
> May come the sound of My feet.
> Therefore I tell you Watch!

God's Anonymous Army

"Yet have I left me seven thousand in Israel." 1 Kings 19:18.

We do well to remind our hearts that there are vastly more unknown than known saints to human fame, both in the Bible and in the history of the church. Elijah had imagined that he was the only remaining champion of the Lord and that the cause might perish if he were killed. But he had to learn that though God had called him to a special task he was not the only loyal servant of Jehovah. Scattered up and down the land were seven thousand obscure individuals whose knees had not bowed to Baal and who were manifesting in less prominent ways their fidelity to God. Elijah has always remained in the limelight, but these others of his time have ever lived in the shadows of obscurity. Because we do not know them, we are in danger of ignoring them.

Is this not also true of the seventy elders appointed to assist Moses and of the seventy disciples Jesus sent forth? If your name has never appeared in print, take courage. The known and famous are in the minority, and the unknown majority are the privileged soldiers in God's host of warriors since they outnumber the generals and captains we know. Never forget that much of the Bible itself was written by God's anonymous scribes. How much poorer the Bible would be without those books whose human authors are unknown.

What would the church do without the majority who render anonymous service? God does not forget the army of quiet helpers upon whom any pastor relies and who manifest fidelity and integrity in their daily lives and are ever ready to serve him. They may be unknown to the world, yet well known to God they have the assurance that his approval is their highest reward. Alexander Pope wrote of one who was "content to breathe his native air" and "live, unseen, unknown." If prayer is the native air we breathe, recognition and fame will not trouble us.